The Illustrated Library of SACRED IMAGINATION

General Editor: Jill Purce

Elémire Zolla

the androgyne

Reconciliation of male and female

with 130 illustrations, 15 in colour

CROSSROAD · NEW YORK

In this series the images and symbols of the
spiritual journey are explored in word and
picture, colour and form. Ancient knowledge,
eternal myth and lost traditions become a new
resource for the human venture. Some of today's
most important religious authors undertake
vision quests and discover authentic sources of
enlightenment and wholeness in oft forgotten
ways. This series constantly and directly points
the spiritually thirsty seeker to the sacred well of
the soul. For there in the heart dwells the creative
imagination. Art and architecture, nature
patterns and life cycles, mystics and their
discoveries become the key to contemplative
living.

© 1981 Thames and Hudson Ltd, London

The Crossroad Publishing Company
575 Lexington Avenue, New York, NY 10022

Library of Congress Catalog Card Number
81–67701

Printed in Japan

Contents

'We two being one, are it.'

(John Donne, 'The Canonization',
in *The Poems of John Donne*,
London, 1933.)

The stalking archetype

The androgyne is stalking through the land. Men feel its shadow on them and relent, cease to cling to their harsh, cramped male roles and persuasions. Women it awakens to neat, icily defined new spaces, to precisely coordinated planes, into which they start calmly picking their way.

Within a metaphysical perspective the encounter with the androgyne has always been unavoidable. When the mind soars above names and forms, it must come to the point where sexual divisions are also bypassed. On their way to total transcendence, mystics go through the hallucinatory experience of divine love and marriage, in which they become the ravished spouses of the godhead.

The androgyne is the symbol of supreme identity in most religious systems. It stands for the level of non-manifested being, the source of manifestation, which corresponds numerically to zero, the most dynamic and puzzling of numbers, the sum of both aspects of Oneness: $+1 - 1 = 0$. Zero symbolizes androgyny as the starting point of numeration, divisibility and multiplicability.

In Hindu metaphysics the polarity of being, represented by Śiva and Śakti, on a higher level becomes sheer unity and blends in the androgyne Ardhanārīśvara. In the *Śatapatha Brahmana* gods and demons engage in a contest. The god Indra says 'One' in the masculine form (*eka*), and the demons answer 'One' in the feminine (*ekā*). Indra says 'Two', masculine dual (*dvau*), and they answer in the feminine dual (*dve*). When five comes up (*pañca*), the devils are silenced. Five is above gender; it contains both odd and even $(3 + 2)$, divisiveness and contrast; with five the four quarters centre $(4 + 1)$ on the heart. Five symbolizes the androgyne as an achievement, as a return from polarity to unity (see also p. 69).

Drawn down from the realm of metaphysical premises to the fluctuating, psychic level of existence, and to the present context, the archetype will suggest something like the elfin world of Belinda's attendants in *The Rape of the Lock* (*Poems*, London, 1939, I, 69–70):

> *For spirits, freed from mortal laws, with ease*
> *Assume what sexes and what shapes they please.*

A programme Virginia Woolf's *Orlando* seemed to fulfil in his/her fluidly perceptive, suave discontinuity.

Dionysus, here represented both as a man and as a woman, was also called the Erect, the Betesticled, the Hybrid, the Man-Woman. In Dionysian frenzy, the devotee identified himself with every aspect of nature, becoming similar to a hermaphrodite plant, capable both of flowering and bearing fruit, of circularly giving and receiving the seed of life and light. (Terracotta busts, Greece, 4th c. BC.)

Today, as family ties wither and the work-ethic declines, their place is being taken by the ideal of a nomadic life of free-floating attachments, of probings into religious experiences and metaphysical teachings. The new hero remains unidentified with roles and is ever ready to trance off onto unusual levels of being. He can suspend the use of conceptual, binary framings, and can therefore stand non-dual situations of maximum symmetry, such as prevail in 'post-modernist' fiction. He feels no anxiety over hybrids, he can even listen calmly to the metaphysician tell him that

> *Far or forgot to* him *is near,*
> *Shadow and sunlight are the same,*
> *One to* him *are shame and fame.*

(R. W. Emerson, *Brahma*,
in *Complete Works*, Boston, 1903–04.)

There develops a capacity for entering into situations and slipping out of them with ease and smoothness, unjudgingly, sedately. He accepts the invitation of Yeats's *Into the Twilight*:

> *Out-worn heart, in a time out-worn,*
> *Come clear of the nets of wrong and right;*
> *Laugh, heart, again in the gray twilight,*
> *Sigh, heart, again in the dew of the morn!*

(in *Collected Poems*, London, 1950.)

In this changed atmosphere, the androgyne has ceased to alarm. The giggles and the hisses at creatures 'of sex indeterminate' fade off into the country we are fast leaving behind us. In fact the unmitigated male or female might soon seem disturbing, a stifling denial of latencies. The model of a well-tempered androgyny hovers above either sex as the new criterion for both, as the incarnation of Cosmic Man.

All this came to the fore at the end of the drug revolution, in the early 1970s, when the leader of the planned subversion of inner space, Timothy Leary, realized that the path of LSD would end in shambles unless androgyny took over. He discovered that it was only if you could face unleashed randomness from what he called a gyroscopic male-female linkage, that you could avoid turning into a babbling acid freak.

At the end of the 1970s the sage of the day, Rajneesh, was offering in his retreat drugless courses in heart-centred androgyny. There people left their shoes and mind at the door, drifted through Tantric sex, if they had to pay their debt to the sex-obsessed world they came from, and finally reached the state of mind where there is no grasping, but only stroking, where one no longer fixates on words, but feels their sweep, dips into the gaps between them, where blue-prints are no longer of any use and where life is steered by womb-deep sympathies. At this point there is nothing to fear. One has Buddha's example of a femininity developed beyond that of any female. Rajneesh says, explaining the secrets of balance, that it is he that is haunted by sin who chooses virtue, he that programmes beauty who is beset with ugliness. Choice is masculine top-heaviness, the androgyne allows life to be unintentional, lets things happen. The complete androgyne wades blissfully through the world of change, *samsara*, balancing action and inactivity.

Jungians have also been trying out formulations of the archetype. James Hillman, the arch-advocate of androgyny, dares cut down to size modern science in favour of an androgynous, non-bisecting sense of the archetypal. Archetypes are too vastly significant to be rudely exposed to raw reasoning, to either-ors. They participate in slow, hidden-up, tucked-in femininity.

Hillman draws up an apology for hysteria, the inevitable price of a stark division of the sexes. Only the wisdom of the god of ecstasy, Dionysus, is actually beyond hysteria. Dionysus takes it in his stride.

If we observe the behaviour of Freud's hysterical patients, we notice that they were vainly trying to intimate to him the secret cause of their condition: for example, the woman who acted out rape during a fit, one hand pressing her skirt down and the other ripping it off. The most famous of Freud's patients, Schreber, wondered obsessively how women must feel, until he imagined himself to be God's wife and spun out the mad minutiae of a sustaining theology.

The power that can heal is not dry reason, but plastic imagination, which is the very dwelling place of the psyche, not merely one of its faculties. Healing does not imply stiff, crude, binary selection, but the relaxing into what Jung would have called a synchronic field, in which psychic peak moments and outer events relating to them are spliced and form luminous clusters of outward-and-inward, of reasoning-and-emotional, of male-and-female experience. At this point the tenet of evolutionary, rationalizing progress (spelt prograss during the drug revolution) vanishes from the scene after an interminable aeon of ruthless supremacy.

Literary incarnations

Literature is the heart's looking-glass, which style seeks to keep speckless. Modern fiction mirrored the androgyne with Théophile Gautier's *Mademoiselle de Maupin* (1835–36), a frail Parisian Romantic variation of *As You Like It*. Mademoiselle wants to 'anatomize' the world of men, so she sets forth on horseback dressed as a young blade. She has made up her mind to keep all her cat-like qualities for her lovers, while displaying dash and passion with her mistresses. Finally she offers a young man the best of both worlds during an unsurpassable night of blended boldness and grace, only to leave on horseback the next morning, since such prodigies cannot endure in a humdrum, bisected everyday world.

Balzac went deeper. His *Séraphita* (1835) tells the story of a youth who first appears with the name of Séraphitus, and captivates both a girl and her fiancé. The sketchy action takes place in a Norwegian valley. The idea of androgyny is conveyed by insistence on the crystal-clear air, on the awesome silence of ice and snow. Séraphitus seems as if of ice, and yet to approach him is to feel all one's nerve-endings vibrate. To him Nature is but a spring-board into an unfathomable beyond. His flower is the azure saxifrage. (See also pp. 94–95.)

A few other, mostly miserable, efforts to seize the archetype were made later on in the century. Only Robert Musil succeeded in capturing it in all its complexity, daring the undared, straining language to the thinnest in *The Man Without Qualities*, which he wrote between 1898 and 1942. He had learnt the lesson of Goethe's androgynes, of which the most poignant and strangely haunting is the pathetic, over-sensitive, boyish Mignon, born in a far-away country of gardens and groves beneath the sunlit, snowcapped Alps. She is kidnapped and turned into a poor little contortionist who trips blindfold through a pile of eggs, and warbles in a heart-rending yet elusive medley of tongues. Also, on the highest level of human existence, there are Wilhelm Meister's 'astral' ladies, who soar above all worldly and fleshly opposites.

Musil has all this behind him, when he introduces us to the 'man without qualities', Ulrich, a young Viennese mathematician. When his father dies, Ulrich returns home; there to meet again, after many years, his sister Agathe. They enter the parlour from opposite sides at the very same moment, symmetrically. Each of them happens to be dressed in the same chequered pyjamas, and looks like a Pierrot, the dazed, lunar, even murderous French version of Polichinello, the hermaphrodite of Neapolitan carnivals (see also pp. 90–91). Still in their strange costumes, Ulrich and Agathe pay their last respects to their father's corpse and then sit down to dinner.

Agathe, Ulrich perceives on close scrutiny, is neither an 'emancipated woman' nor a 'bohemian', but rather, a hermaphrodite. Her body is as though enfolded by a layer of water. And it is as though out of deep waters that he emerges the next morning from his sleep. He is obsessed by strange questions: 'Why has water three states, liquid, solid, gaseous, and man only two, solid male and liquid female? Why does Nature foist nipples on men, clitorises on women?'

When brother and sister take a stroll, they feel that all their ambitions are dropping away, and a slumbering mellowness is taking their place. They decide to live together.

Agathe now appears to her brother like a moon peeping over the next roof-top. When he helps her dress after her bath, he feels that although he is in his own body, he is also in touch with a more beautiful one, which is, however, equally his own. Now, when the two of them walk through the streets, people stare and seem strangely moved, but at the same time are tempted to make fun of them. They represent the intolerable mysteries of creation, the hermaphrodite, Isis-Osiris, the same and the other, the mirror and the mirrored. They are disturbing, like a lady suddenly appearing undressed, or a nude dancer turning up somewhere else fully clothed.

Their shared life fans out into a myriad ecstasies, like a peacock's tail spreading out into eyes. When they fall into one another's arms, they hold back not for moral reasons, but either in obedience to an order 'from the world of the most perfect conjunction' or for some unfathomable intimation or out of curiosity at what is happening to them at that precise moment. Their dazzling sensuality is impersonal, all one with the moon-flooded garden outside, with its silvery lawn, with the curving limbs of the apple tree, its silence broken by the crackling of hidden ice – the inevitable ice of an androgyne scenario. The only words that now seem fit for them to use in describing what is happening to them are passages from the supreme mystics, from Meister Eckhart or Suso: their hearts are bottomless, their loving souls are loveless, their natures unreal. They are madly in love, but know not with whom, being beyond names and forms.

They next leave on a holiday, and embrace on the balcony of a hotel room overlooking the Adriatic, feeling that they are bending the horizon round their loins. It is as though they are taking a leap, falling into the void and being sustained by the sheer intensity of their happiness, which is almost like sadness.

When Agathe opens her eyes, she perceives the starlit body of her brother as near as the surrounding shadows and as distant as the stars, but he now exists within her. She feels at peace, with her heart rolled up like a mummy – the same image that occurs to Virginia Woolf's Orlando when he/she climaxes into having a baby, and falls into a sleep, a sleep in which all shapes are ground into a dim liquid softness – like a folded, shrouded mummy.

Agathe's and Ulrich's world has become timeless, symmetrical and indescribable – the realm of twins, doubles, androgynes, where there exists neither before nor after, neither right nor left. When they look at something, they blend into it, as wine mixes with water. The scene is now set for the descent and the revelation of the archetype.

Agathe notices that she has left her body. She sees it stretched out naked on the bed, the pale tuft of hairs like a golden flame on a marble slab. They both find themselves looking down at her body in wonder. To two in one, all experiences are similes. They feel as if they are on fire. They are the androgyne. Musil wrote no farther.

Other attempts at describing the androgyne seem tame by comparison, as when the theme emerges in American Southern Gothic fiction, with Carson McCullers, or with Flannery O'Connor, who dared compare the display of a hermaphrodite freak at a fair with the raising of the Host at Mass (in *A Temple of the Holy Ghost*, 1954).

But recently one step further has been taken; the androgynous mysteries of sorcery have been laid open in Carlos Castaneda's *The Second Ring of Power* (1978). Five sorceresses are pitted against Carlos, a green warlock, fresh from initiation, amid barren, menacing Mexican mountains. The women need a new master wizard, whom they can select only by fighting him, through challenge and defiance. The women must seek to wrest out of him by deceit or assault the portion of the Sun which he has absorbed. And only by flourishing fierce, invisible dream-like limbs, can he, the prospective leader, withstand the test. He must hit back at each vicious, sly stroke of his future subjects, who need him so badly to balance their wild energy of wind-dominated, wind-riding witches. They need his subtle, unconscious maleness to balance themselves with. He in turn requires the stimulus of their allurements and cruelties, to make his double, his dream body burn and flash out, a force for destruction and for healing. Their common aim is to become one, blending into a single cluster of luminescent fibres, as happened with Ulrich and Agathe. 'We are the same' is the strange, tantalizing war-cry which echoes all through the ordeal. At the end Carlos and the most complete sorceress of the group for a short interval seem to clinch and actually become One.

The archaic triads

What Cosmic jest or Anarch blunder
The human integral clove asunder
And shied the fractions through life's gate?

(Herman Melville, *After the Pleasure-party*,
in *Collected Poems*, New York, 1964.)

There is a strange archaic ring about Melville's question. So keenly was its urgency felt in many ancient civilizations that their cosmogonies were fashioned to suit. Their statements about the primal mystery of being, their narratives of the origin of the world, aimed at answering first of all that central, obsessive query.

That man was in origin created androgyne – Plato's solution in the *Symposium* – is paralleled all over the world. At the beginning of time men had been balls or discs, rolled up, egg-shaped or star-like androgynes. Plato was writing in the relaxed Athenian atmosphere, so he figured out androgyne primordials for everyone. What blending might Alcibiades long for, who looked so wooingly on old Socrates? What completion might tempt a lady haunted by the poignant suggestions and sweet majesty of Sappho's songs? So in the *Symposium* three primordials are imagined: the androgyne proper – man and woman coupled like the serpents of Hermes' caduceus – and the two homosexual matings.

In India the androgyne is usually conceived as Śiva and his consort Parvati fused into one being. But there also exists a male-to-male link, at least among Śivaites. The gods and the demons, it is said, were fighting for the beverage of immortality, and during the contest Śiva fell in love with Mohini, the androgynous arch-seductress. He discovered that she was Viṣṇu-Hari in disguise, but, undaunted, embraced her-him with such violence that they became one (bibliography in Daniélou 1960, p. 284).

Eroticism becomes a serious affair when it turns into magic. According to certain archaic systems there are three kinds of magic: the magic of fertility, of warfare and of spells, which correspond to the three spheres – of earth and production; of winds, passion and warfare; and finally of the high skies or of the nether-world, from where exorcisms work and curses bind.

Plato's three primordials might fit into this frame. Man-to-woman love has always been connected with nature's bounty, while male homosexuality is akin to warfare and to what was, like the performing arts, traditionally linked to the warrior caste. To some temperaments this is the only conceivable completion. (Sir Thomas Browne, in his considerations on hermaphrodites in *Pseudodoxia epidemica*, 1646, wrote that Eve was surely fashioned out of Adam's rib for the sake of reproduction, because had it been for companionship, a male would have been preferable.) The Russian Orthodox Church created a ritual for the consecration of male friendship, which in our time Father Pavel Florenskij intended to revive. Among the Nzemas of Ghana and the Nubas in Sudan, marriage among males is institutionalized; it implies passionate attraction, even rapture, but not intercourse (see Signorini 1973). Among American Indians, most male married couples originate from a shamanic calling, which has almost turned one of the partners physically into a woman.

In India, the transvestite performers called on for weddings and feasts lead an epicene (dual sexual) life. Their god is Kumāra, the Youth, who in Bengal is also the god of thieves. Born of Śiva's sperm, he was brought up by the Pleiades (Krittikas) and is hence called Kārtikeya. He leads the army of the gods. His lady is the army; women in some versions of his myth he rejects (bibliography in Daniélou 1960, pp. 452–56).

According to a legend which circulates among these transvestites, Śiva and his consort Parvati decide one day to give wives to their sons Ganesha (Wisdom) and Kārtikeya (Valour), and request of them an action of thanksgiving. Kārtikeya decides to encircle the world on his peacock. Ganesha's mount is the tiny mouse, so he decides instead to circle round the essence of the world, his divine parents. They are so flattered, that they bestow both brides on him. When weary Kārtikeya comes home from his cosmic circumambulation, and sees from afar the two fires of the brother's double marriage, he decides to eschew womanhood henceforth. Women are therefore not allowed into his temples.

Kārtikeya is the god of strength; he plants his spear in the earth, and, as with Excalibur in the Arthurian cycle, nobody else can extract it. His banner is red, it evokes the destruction of the world. He is also known as Subrahmanya, ('Dear-to-Brahmins') or as Śarabhū ('Born-of-a-fount'). Mystically he is the power of the seed when it is drawn up into the brain through the central, androgyne artery (suśumnā). In honour of Subrahmanya, boys in southern India subject themselves to self-torture, enter fire-pits and walk over embers. He grants them immunity to pain. Subrahmanya assists the soul in its magical expeditions out of the body.

In ancient Greece, pederasty was a military custom, and a warrior's cult of Eros developed (see Fasce 1977). The two child gods, Eros and Anteros, 'Love' and 'Requital-of-love', or 'Turn-over', were imagined locked in fights and embraces.

The mythical link between Eros and war makes military campaigns into battles of love. In consequence, war has often meant the defloration of the vanquished. This custom was scrupulously practised by the Langobard invaders of the Roman Empire. The mythic fixation seems ineradicable and lives on through the ages in the subconscious, stronger than if it were taught and cultivated in temples: soldiers and criminals still go through its obsessive, endless litanies about the erotic treatment to be meted out to imaginary foes. No religious chants anywhere are repeated so untiringly or with such dedication as these, in barracks and in prisons. Little brats pick them up as soon as they enter school.

It is extremely difficult to come by couples of loving women initiates. Theirs should be the purely heavenly or nether-worldly marriage. The Greek geographer Strabo took it for granted that women are by nature closer to the sphere of religion. According to the Swiss jurist Johannes Bachofen, a general social and religious change took place with the downfall of Amazonian societies, when female priestesses were obliged to hand down their learning to men, as Medea did to Jason. It was, however, through a priestess (Diotima) that Socrates received initiation. Dionysian cults reasserted the role of women initiators in a male-dominated society. Couples of Celtic priestesses granted initiation to heroes, and in the Irish Echtrae stories, the Land of the Living, or Other World, where time becomes vaster and sweet peace reigns, is a land of women. Female priesthood is here deliberately contrasted with Druidism.

The Norse Valkyries, like the divine maids of Turkic shamanic peoples, are imagined in mythological songs as a college of swan-priestesses. They mediate between the warriors and Odin, the god of magic, of wisdom-through-frenzy, who acquired his powers through 'unmanly rites'. The Valkyries possess the knowledge of runes and of magic beverages. Through hierogamy (sacred marriage) with them, heroes reach immortality.

Two female couples stand out in the annals of shamanism (see also Halifax 1979, pp. 25–28). In North America, 'Manlike Woman', an early nineteenth-century Kootenai, followed orders received in dreams and left her husband to marry a woman. She became a great prophet; it was she who foretold the end of the Indian way of life. There is also a memorable story of an old Eskimo woman with an adopted daughter, who, when her tribe forsook her, turned herself into a man and married the daughter. With her sexual magic she attracted seals and caribou and drew foxes to her den.

To return to Plato's primordial couples, the ideal temple was the place where, if not all three, the first two would come to life in peculiar rites. The temples of the ancient Middle East shocked the Biblical prophets with their displays of male and female practitioners of erotic magic ('the dogs! the bitches!').

A shrine is a display of archetypes. In the great surviving Hindu temples, the thrill can still be felt of meeting *the* white horse, *the* divine elephant, *the* sacred monkeys, *the* fish which purify their temple tank to the last speck, *the* icons of all imaginable cosmic energies lined up under the black vaults, and finally, behind a painted veil, behind *māyā*, in the innermost recess, the male *lingam* ritually washed with lime juice, anointed with sandalwood, eternally at one with the female *yoni* – two in one. The priesthood of olden times comprised both female and male dancers and singers, and particular hierogamies were the culmination of their services; these represented the archetypes of androgyny.

Shamanic wounds

Temple practices are the shamanic, metaphysical secrets of the bush, desert retreat, cavern or forest transposed to man-made settings.

Shamans become androgynous by mating with a partner – in the flesh or in fantasy, or by transcending their sex in the intensity of their rapture.

In the songs of the Mazatec shamaness María Sabina, one of the most interesting documents culled from the poor remains of shamanism, the process of her androgynization can be followed step by step, as the sacred mushroom takes effect, progressively expanding her consciousness. She intones a paean of self-glorification:

> I am María Sabina. She is the woman who bides her time, she is the woman who probes, she is the woman of victory; she is the woman of thought, the woman who creates, she is the woman who cures, she is the Sun woman, the Moon woman, the woman who interprets . . . The sacred mushroom takes me to the world where everything is known . . . The mushroom is like the soul. Where the soul wants to go, it takes you.

> (Halifax 1979, p. 130; translation slightly modified.)

Next María Sabina rises above opposites:

> *Woman like the big eagle am I.*
> *Woman like the opossum am I.*
> *And woman like the wolf am I.*
> *Woman like the hunting dog am I.*
> *I'll show my power.*
> *Male saint I am.*
> *Woman of pure spirit*
> *I shall disenchant*
> . . . .
>
> *Man who stays and stands, and*
> *Woman root below water am I.*
> . . . .
>
> *Whirling woman*
> *In the whirlwind I am.*
> *Male saint I am.*
> *It's a holy man, says [the mushroom].*
> *It's a holy woman, says [the mushroom].*

> (Halifax 1979, p. 198; translation slightly modified.)

'Santo-santa, santo-santa' becomes an incantation – feeling her/himself to be both a male and a female saint helps the shaman rise above human, limited existence. Sometimes he/she is helped by a dream bride or bridegroom. In either case the dream experience may have strange effects on the practitioner's sex.

The mystical poets of the Italian thirteenth-century *Stilnovo* called themselves women and it probably ended there, but it is known that Lamaist practitioners can identify with their ladies or *dakinis* (female deities) by dint of hallucinating on them.

The apprentice and the supernatural helper are usually of opposite sexes, and the apprentice will take on the sex of the helper. Sometimes the metaphor is even lived out in everyday life. Among the Dayaks in Celebes, the Araucanians in Chile, the Chukchees in Siberia, as among many North American tribes, an actual, total, often agonizing switch of sexual habits would take place (see Baumann 1955). The shaman is a creature of the crossroads, and in order to seize the currents of energy, he/she places him/herself where they join – as María Sabina places herself between the opossum and the eagle, the wolf and the hunting dog, the waterlily's upright male stalk and curved female underwater root. The price can be frightful.

The reasons given for the inversion are varied and complex. In the cult of Cybele the devotee's identification with the Mother's Son and Lover was wrought to such a pitch as he span round and round, whirling his head and crying aloud, that he finally slit off his sex as an offering to her. It was embalmed, probably painted gold, draped in his last male tunic and placed on the goddess's bed. The devotee would henceforth don a chaste yellow robe in which he awaited death, when he would retrieve his sex and become an androgyne.

Eunuchs have always been masters of song and dance, mediators in worship, and counsellors to the throne. Their presence was still thought necessary at the Chinese Court at the beginning of this century, and at the Sistine Chapel in the Vatican not much earlier.

Circumcision – as well as clitoridectomy – is sometimes, as among the Dogons, motivated by a desire to remove the traces of androgyny. However it matters little whether the obsession with androgyny pretends to be disdain instead of attraction. At its heart, circumcision is the token of a mitigated, spiritualized androgyny – the sign of 'eunuchs for the Kingdom'. Among the Hereros of South Africa, who wear the clothes of the opposite sex in their ancestor worship, the primordial, mystical motivation is maintained and the circumcised are called 'male virgins'.

The foreskin is seen as a marriage ring, or as a crown offered to a god; the sticky blood which pours from the cut strengthens the link. Blood grips sawdust like a vice, turns it into timber as hard as teak. It should seal hard pacts.

The Scythians – who, Herodotus recounts, howled in their hemp steam-baths – were supposed to attain physical androgyny by constantly riding over their small horses' necks, amongst other practices. Those who achieved the goal were prayed to. The Amazons were Scythian women who became one with their steeds and achieved androgyny by scorching or removing their right breast, not only for archery, but to acquire a symmetrical androgyny (like that of the Hindu Ardhanārīśvara, the double-sexed Śiva), making male the right-hand side of their bodies.

The archetype of the androgyne can become a hard, bloodthirsty taskmaster. This is apparent at its – to us – most horrifying in the subincision ceremonies of Australian aborigines. After circumcision, a cut is made into the lower part of the penis, baring the urethra. The opening is periodically made to bleed as proof of the adept's link with the source of life and with the central archetype of the androgyne, visibly manifested in the star Delta Scorpionis or in the Rainbowsnake (see p. 67). All nature is set in motion by Rainbowsnake, and the supreme mystical goal is to identify with it. This implies becoming androgyne, and submitting to subincision after circumcision. One myth relates that the Wangeluk sisters (whose name means both 'womb' and 'subincision') sought to prevent Rainbowsnake's downpours, and were swallowed up by him. He soon regretted the meal, but discovered that when he spoke, it was with the voices and wisdom of

圖 胎 道

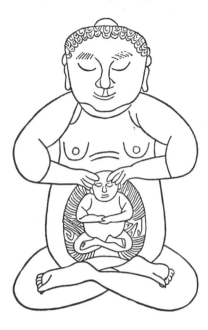

The foetus of immortality, which Taoist adepts slowly develop by balancing their male and female energies and gathering them into the field of the androgyne – utterly stable power, visualized beneath the navel. The foetus grows into a new subtle body of light, with which the adept will identify, leaving behind his body of flesh, just as an insect, ceasing to be a grub, abandons its chrysalis and turns into a pure imago. (Woodcut from Lu K'uan Yü, Taoist Yoga, Alchemy and Immortality, London, 1970.)

the sisters. He then passed on to his offspring the esoteric androgyne lore that he had acquired.

Taoism and Tantra

Androgyny can be an inner goal. The opposite parts of the soul then come together like a man and woman in ecstatic love-making.

The inner sexual duality has nearly always been taken for granted. Shakespeare explains:

> *My brain I'll prove the female to my soul;*
> *My soul, the father: and these two beget*
> *A generation of still-breeding thoughts,*
> *And these same thoughts people this little world*
> *In humours like the people of this world.*

(*Richard II*, V, iv, 8–12.)

A harmonious human being balances father-soul and matrix-brain, peopling his or her little world with spherical, star-like androgynous thoughts.

A strongly sexed inner imaginative process leading to this realization is preserved in many mystical paths. There is much evidence of it in Taoism (see Van Gulik 1961, Lu K'uan Yü 1970 and Bichen 1979), in Hindu Tantrism and in Vajra Buddhism (see Snellgrove 1959, Blofeld 1978/79 and Chen 1968).

Taoist techniques, aimed at developing the female spirit 'of the valley' or 'of the abyss' (see also pp. 68–69), direct the practitioner to visualize his breath as being stored up in his belly, and then condensed into a golden drop of concentrated light about three inches (7–8 cm) below his navel. The drop of light can even be projected as the ideogram of brightness, of the circulation of light, sun-and-moon. □ 日 It can also be seen as an embryo that is progressively developed and nourished. It is made to ascend to the head through equalizing the male sun-breath and the female moon-breath, the two spiralling currents or serpents of energy (in Sanskrit the iḍa/piṅgala currents) which are alternately propelled by rolling the closed eyes clockwise and then counter-clockwise like windmills. All the time the curled tongue is kept pressed up against the palate like an axle. It can also be employed to write the ideogram on the vault of the palate. When this practice is followed by a man during intercourse, the force of female erotic stimulation is brought to bear, as an additional spur to the process, on the drop of light in the abdomen, and it acts like water sprinkled on blazing oil or phosphorus. At the acme, the back is bent back, shoulders are squared, breath is held, and the eyes roll with a wild stare. Intercourse can be used both by a man and by a woman to balance their energies and 'immortalize' themselves.

This peak of bliss and knowledge was attained by the Eight Taoist Immortals. Among them is Lan Ts'ai Ho, both man and woman. He-she appeared out of the blue, one foot shod, the other bare, with a wooden belt

Lan Ts'ai Ho. (Woodcut, China.)

at his-her waist, dancing with a basket of flowers in one hand and singing about the fleeting nature of all things:

> *In the morning I ride in the sky,*
> *In the evening I see the mulberry groves turn into a sea.*
> *Our hope is in the clouds;*
> *There you shall find palaces of silver and gold.*

(T. C. Lai, The Eight Immortals, Hong Kong, 1972.)

Lan Ts'ai Ho was always tipsy and would make people collapse with laughter. He-she wore heavy clothing in the summer and light dress in the winter, when he-she would sleep in the snow, surrounded by a beautiful mist. He-she never aged, but one day, while drinking in a tavern, he-she heard the sound of music and rose to heaven, where he-she disappeared, casting off his-her dress, one shoe, wooden belt and castanets.

In a probably later legend, P'an Hu, who created the world out of Yang and Yin, sought incarnation in a virgin hermaphrodite hermit, living on the essence of sun and moon upon a mountain. She gave birth to him from her spinal column and was named the Mother of the First Cause.

Hindu scriptures establish the same principles as those of Taoism, though their techniques vary. Intercourse, they state, is of magic benefit essentially to the woman, but the man can turn the tables on her by visualizing the act as a sacrifice, in which the womb serves as an altar. The *Mahābhārata* mentions female ascetics who turn themselves into males – such as Amba, who became Arjuna's charioteer. (Joan of Arc was reviving a forgotten myth.)

Tantrism developed into *vajra* (diamond, lightning or phallus) Buddhism. *Vajra* love is supposed to follow the use, first of the spiritual method called the 'small vehicle' (in which women's bodies are visualized as putrefied corpses), and then of the 'big vehicle', in which the very roots of desire are annihilated in the ecstasy (*samadhi*) of voidness (*sunyatā*). Now at last the mystic is ready for the *vajra* games of love, in which pleasure is a metaphor of voidness. There is a minor void he reaches through self-effacing absorption in his partner, a major void attained by letting himself float upon the waves of pleasure, and finally, the 'resonance of pleasure', in which the red and the white seeds of female and male – the subtle sensation or counterpart of the two reproductive fluids – coalesce, and the androgyne or embryo is born. Now the light of the higher world, of *dharmakaya*, appears. The art of prolonging this enlightenment leads to immortality. When the two serpents or contrary flows of energy – sun and moon, semen and blood, the symbols of masculine endeavour or compassion and female void – are balanced, compassion can no longer be a delusion, nor voidness mere apathy: they flow together.

Snake-charmers in India were originally Tantric masters, and their music acted on the inner serpents. It also provoked a phallic arousal which was probably that of the dreaming state (of REM sleep) rather than that of sex.

In Buddhism, meditation sometimes focuses on the Lord Buddha's retractile penis. Visualizations are also practised whereby the Green Lady or Tārā of Compassion (Avalokiteśvara) is contracted to an emerald drop of

The male Avalokiteśvara is here transforming into the compassionate Lady Kuan Yin, as he-she is overwhelmed by his-her motherly love for little children (her devotees). Soon, however, she will be ready to change back into her male form, becoming a fierce general in order to defend his devotees in the Chinese hell. (Statue by Wang Tsun-yeh, China, 6th C. AD.)

beaming splendour, which enters the meditator's head and descends into his heart. He then starts seeing his body shrink until it becomes the size of Tārā – and in fact becomes her. Apparently old monks practising the visualization looked distinctly androgynous (see Blofeld 1978/79).

In mystical love lyrics all over the world, the poet faints and sobs like a woman before an unyielding god-like mistress who is his higher self. The tradition runs from Siberian shamans to Taoist Chinese poets, through Iran, Arabia, Provence, to the Florentine *Stilnovo* poets who called themselves 'women'.

Dante describes how one should build up in one's mind the image of the Lady, and hallucinate on her, just as Tantrikas do on their Devis or Tārās. Finally one achieves the transformation described in *Paradiso* I. 67–71: 'gazing on her, such [as she] I became within; as happened with Glaucus [the Greek boy who took the sacred plunge] after having tasted the weed that made him in the sea fellow of the other Gods. To pass beyond the human could not be told in words, but illustration will do, for him whom experience grace'.

The same process appears in Tamil texts: the amazonian goddesses embody 'the principle of exchange', absorbing the devotee's masculinity as he proceeds through a symbolic castration, until they merge (see Schulman 1977). Then, in Dante's words, the renewed man can 'take his pleasure for his leader' (*Purgatorio* XXVII), and bestow a crown and mitre on himself, that is, assume the supreme secular and spiritual authority, becoming Cosmic Man and Cosmic Woman.

Greek and Indian mythology

Precious little is known of what was whispered at mysteries and behind temple doors in Greece. Many myths, however, would make added sense against a background of Tantric-like practices. This is so with one of the episodes in the Hercules myth.

After having slain the son of Eurytus, Hercules is contaminated, unbalanced, and Hermes takes him in charge, selling him in bondage to Queen Omphale (Omphalos means 'the navel', the place in the body where Eastern practitioners locate man's 'Herculean' energies). His first feat in her

Orpheus as a woman, playing the lyre, surrounded by demons brandishing serpents.

service consists in killing a serpent and takes place near the river Sangarios, where a man who had derided the eunuchs of the Mother of the Gods had drowned himself in despair at his sin. After completing the deed, Hercules is released by the Queen. He is now an androgyne. At night he makes love to the Queen and during the day he lives and dresses as a girl. Pan even tries his luck with him, one night when he and the Queen happen to be sleeping separately. At the end of the episode, Hercules appears perfectly purified and balanced.

Another story that seems to hint at Tantric practices is that of Agdystis, born of a drop of Zeus' semen that, according to one version, had fallen upon a stone, or according to another, that Zeus had spilt while trying to rape Cybele. Agdystis is androgyne; the gods fear such double power and deprive him/her of his/her testicles. From these the almond tree of life springs, covered with ripe almonds. A daughter of the Sangarios river is impregnated in the process, and gives birth to Attis. A complicated, unhappy love affair follows between Agdystis and Attis, ending in Attis' emasculation. In general, stories in which normal love is thwarted and different goals are substituted hint at Tantric practices, as in the case of androgyne Orpheus, slain by the women who had been infuriated by his aloofness.

Such stories all belong to the general mythical pattern which has been called the 'Joseph-Potiphar's wife motif' (from the story in Genesis 39): a beautiful youth behaves chastely towards a lady, who is often his step-mother (see Johanaan 1968). One of its versions is the story of Hippolytus and Phaedra, in which, as appears from Euripides' play, the youth is an initiate of double-sexed Orphic Iacchus, and his step-mother Phaedra is described as an Amazon. In the Buddhist legend *The Eyes of Kunala*, we probably have the original story: the chaste youth closes his ears to the woman's entreaties, and she has him blinded out of spite. But by losing his fleshly sight he gains supernatural insight.

This leads to another set of Greek myths based on blinding and illumination, the stories of Teiresias.

Teiresias, as a girl of seven, is taught music by Apollo in exchange for her love, but once she has learnt, she denies him her favours. He turns her into a boy; Zeus and Hera, unable to agree on whether it is the man or the woman who most enjoys love-making, turn to Teiresias for his verdict. The stripling answers that woman enjoys it nine times more than man. Hera, enraged at having lost the argument, turns him back into a woman. A boy beloved of Poseidon then tries to make love to Teiresias while she is bathing in a pool, and she wounds him. Poseidon in revenge turns her back into a man again. Teiresias next slights Aphrodite by denying her a beauty prize, and in punishment is turned into an old crone. In spite of her age Teiresias becomes the lover of Spider-Man (Arachnos), who gives *her* the nick-name of Aphrodite. This the goddess Aphrodite cannot brook, so she changes Spider-Man into a weasel and Teiresias into a mouse (which in Greece is the animal of Apollo, from whom all the story started and in India the mount of the god of wisdom, Ganesha).

In another version Teiresias as a man sees two serpents mating, strikes the female with his staff and is himself turned into a female. Later she comes across the same scene once more, and this time strikes the male, regaining her masculinity. *Vajra* sex in an allegorical nut-shell. One day Teiresias surprises Artemis the Moon taking a bath, and is punished with the loss of his eyesight, but granted prophecy in compensation. Actaeon too happened to catch sight of the goddess bathing, and was turned into a stag (a symbol of supernatural knowledge among shamanic hunting tribes).

In another stray anecdote from the Teiresias cycle, Hera, instead of turning Teiresias into a mouse for his verdict about women's pleasure at sex, strikes him blind.

In India Teiresias' counterpart is Nārada, the sage of sages, whose wisdom, however, falls short of androgyny, the final touch. One day he discovers Viṣṇu and Lakṣmī making love, and chides the god for falling prey to the witchery of *māyā*, cosmic delusion. To teach him a lesson Viṣṇu immerses Nārada in a sacred pool and turns him into a woman (see pp. 86–87). Only when Nārada as a woman and a mother has experienced the grief of seeing all her sons die on the battlefield, does Viṣṇu change her back to a man. Nārada now no longer questions the wisdom of the love-making gods. Only through androgynization can the adept overcome *māyā*, which depends on everything being made of contrary pairs (as the *Bhagavad Gītā* explains, VII:27:28).

In Śivaite lore the same lesson is taught in the story of the Ascetics of the Pine Forest. These are a group of exceptional yogic masters, but they have not attained androgyny, so Śiva appears to them as a beautiful androgyne, the goddess Umā occupying half of his body, or as a lovely youth accompanied by Viṣṇu in female form (see also pp. 74–75). The wives and sons of the ascetics (the feelings and actions of the ascetics?) fall in love with Śiva, and in vain the ascetics curse him; in the end they are even obliged to seek his forgiveness.

Temple dancing girls at Tirucenkottu claim descent from the ascetics' wives. The myth probably provided an explanation for a double priesthood, representing both the wives and the sons of the ascetics who had been converted to the worship of the Śivalingam.

In Greek mythology Teiresias is the pivot of a number of related cycles. First of all in the story of Oedipus, 'Swollen Foot' (see also pp. 88–89). He was born to King Laius of Thebes, who in fear of an oracle predicting the evils to come, lamed him and cast him out into the wilderness. Oedipus survived and grew into a sturdy youth, who one day, without knowing who the man was, killed his father Laius for having run him over and wounded his lame foot with the wheel of the chariot. (According to another version he killed Laius for having abducted his boy lover.) The story goes on to recount that Oedipus next came to the gates of Thebes, where Hera, the guardian of married life, had placed the Sphinx, with orders to lay waste the country in punishment for the king's pederasty. The Sphinx had a woman's face, the body of a lion, the tail of a serpent, the wings of an eagle, possibly representing the four quarters of the year. She was the goddess of death and power. Oedipus overcame her by solving her riddle, 'What is the beast that leans first on four, then on two, and finally on three legs?' His answer was 'Man, on all fours as a child, upright as a man, leaning on a stick in old age'. Oedipus enters Thebes and marries the queen, his own mother. He is now, as Aeschylus tells us, 'the foremost of men', 'similar to the gods'. But blind, groping Teiresias staggers forth, looks straight into his most unguarded secrets and openly reveals them. On learning that he has killed his father and mated with his mother, Oedipus plucks out his eyes, becoming, like Teiresias, a sage.

Another Teiresian offshoot is the story of Narcissus. The river-god Cephissus entwined himself round the water nymph Leiriope, 'She Who Waters the Lily' (see p. 53), siring on her Narcissus. Teiresias was then consulted (for the first time as a seer) and predicted that Narcissus would live only as long as he did not see his own image. Narcissus grew up to be a handsome boy who slighted male and female suitors alike. One day near Helicon he discovered a quiet pool: according to one version he fell in love with his own reflection in the water, his own image acting as a magnet on the female part of himself, or else he thought he saw in the water his beloved dead sister, who had been indistinguishable from himself. He fell into a swoon and was transformed into a narcissus (in Greek the word means 'narcotizer', 'swooner').

All these myths (to which should be added that of Hermaphroditus, described on p. 45), can be considered as belonging to a single cycle, like snatches from one huge opera. They are based, broadly speaking, on the following pattern:

a) Suitors are slighted or a goddess is offended or mating is hindered, the hidden meaning possibly being that an esoteric use is made of sex.

b) A plunge is taken into transforming waters, or contact is made with serpents. The currents of subtle inner energy may be alluded to in either case.

c) There follows a succession of switches in sex; one's self-reflection pivots on its axis of symmetry. In Tantric sex the two opposite currents are usually stimulated in turn.

d) The consequence is a loss of sight leading to the acquisition of spiritual or prophetic insight, or the granting of the gift of music, the mastery of rhythms. In the Narcissus myth the explicit discovery of the self-delusive quality of *māyā* takes the place of the loss of sight.

The Jewish esoteric tradition

Although the androgyne has not played a central role in the Christian West, its hidden ferment has been strangely at work in the dark. The West is a graft on the ancient tree of Israel, from which it so widely differs.

Their Bibles appear to be one and the same, but the Jewish and the Christian readings are worlds apart. Israel, like China, appears as exoterically patriarchal as it is esoterically androgynous, given to careful, untiring balancings. Genesis 1:26 offers the crucial text:

And Elōhīm said – Let us make man [*ādām*, 'the earthly'; *Ādāmāh*, 'earth'] in our image [*tzelem*, 'figure' or 'imagination', and according to Qabbalists also 'destiny' or 'mould', the raiment of light or body of glory, or crown, which was lost with the fall, but which was restored to Moses] and in our likeness and let him rule . . . and Elōhīm created man [ādām] in his image, in the image of Elōhīm created him male and female and blessed them, and Elōhīm said to them – be fruitful, multiply and fill the earth [this was interpreted to mean that Adam extended from heaven to earth].

Image was read as 'man' and likeness as 'woman'; it followed that man shall rule only when in image *and* likeness similar to God (the relevant rabbinical commentary is *Midrash Rabbah* I, c.VIII).

If androgyne Adam is the reflection of God, then God too must be androgyne (an inference which is not, however, specifically drawn in Midrashic rabbinical literature; only in the Qabbalah does God's androgyny come to the fore; see Patai 1978). God as manifestation, in the Qabbalah as in Tantra, is the mating androgyne, the two poles united in absolute bliss. The Hindu parallels are striking: even that Eve is known to the *Tripura Samhita* as Adam's left side ('The wise should know that the female resides in the left side of males'). (For specific links between Qabbalah and Tantra, see Patai 1977.)

In God's name, יהוה (IHVH), the Qabbalist reads י (I) the Father, ה (H) the Mother and וה (VH) the androgyne cosmos or Son-and-Daughter, who were created as joined back-to-back, but in the process of cosmic development are separated and unite face to face. IH is the primal manifestation of divinity, VH the consequent uniting.

Genesis 1:20 is read as: 'Let the waters bring forth the reptile, the living soul [*Khayah*, living creature] – when Father and Mother are joined, in the moving of the water, all things multiply.' IHVH, who does not take part in creation (the creator in Genesis being Elohim), is the male, Elohim the female, the power, the kingdom – *šakti* moulds the shapes of manifestation. The male and female mating are Justice and Judgment, Lenience and Severity, Right and Left, the two opposite rows of branches on the Tree of Life conjoined.

When Elohim decided to split Adam in two, he (or they) plunged him into a kind of death or sleep. Woman was then created from Adam's left side, or, according to some commentators, as his bottom half ('by God visibly adorned and cushioned'). Adam's split was thus made good, and the androgyne re-forms, with man and woman conjoined; the body becomes unified once more, like the Tree of Life 'which feeds all flesh, and the beasts of the field lie in its shade and amid its branches nest the fowls of the air'. Then the emanation of God (called *Yesod*, Foundation, which stands for the phallus, 'the Just one'), penetrates the lower emanation, *Malkuth* (the Kingdom, 'Mercy', the Womb), whose centre is Jerusalem or Justice. The armies of God are the two emanations. Glory (*Hod*) on the left and Victory (*Netzach*) on the right are the testicles gathering consecrated oils from above – from the left-hand emanation of Analysis or severity (*Ghevurah*), and the right-hand one of Synthesis and lenience (*Ghedullah*).

But all blessings, says the *Zohar*, radiate from the male skull, when breath (*hevel*) is not breathed forth – a metaphor for sexual ecstasy – and the white (male) and red (female) seeds unite into one radiance; then 'the just one

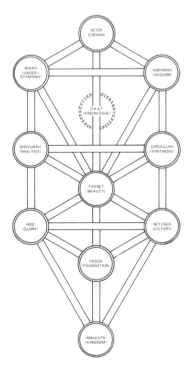

The Tree of Life.

21

brings forth fruit like the palm-tree'. The *lingam* (phallus) becomes hermaphrodite.

It is also possible to find in the *Zohar* all the supporting texts for Musil's variations on the androgyne (see pp. 8–9): 'She clings to the side of the Male, so She is called "My dove, my perfect one" – you read not "my perfect one" [*Thamathi*], but "my twin sister" [*Thamuthi*]' says the *Zohar* (ch. 713) and adds that souls absorbed in the 'divine body' join the just one (the *lingam*) and justice (*yoni*): 'They rise to the disk of the moon, where they see what they see and in their mirth they rise and sink, they come near and separate. The moon attracts them and sheds light . . . ' (Abbé Busson 1895). Even Musil's apple tree answers to the texts of the Qabbalists, who identify God's glory with the apple orchard of the *Song of Songs* (815), where the male and the female conjoin (see Scholem 1980).

Within each individual the two forces are present as soul and reason, heart and brain, and while exoterically the feminine, left force (*yetzer-ra*) is considered by Jewish mystics as evil, esoterically it is taught that the greater his *yetzer-ra*, the greater the man, for as he dominates over it, it becomes his auxiliary – and the perfect man comprises the two harmonized together.

St John the Baptist

St John the Baptist's familiar icon, the severed head on a platter (see also pp. 84–85) is a Hindu symbol for the mating of the sun and moon at the beginning and at the end of time (*Ṛg Veda* 1.110. 3–5). His legend as Baptizer is based on a Jewish version of the motif of the plunge into transforming waters (see also pp. 86–87).

The so-called 'historical' legend recounts that Herodias wanted to pass on to her husband Herod her bewitching daughter by a previous husband, Salomé, who might then have become a second (or nth) wife, but for the contrary verdict of John, the opinionated legalitarian. Herod was maddened by an irresistible dance of little Salomé, or in some versions Herodias herself (the two are often confused), who then refused him her favours unless he gave her the prophet's head as a present. But it was known that if the blood of a holy man was spilt on the earth the crops would wither, so the head was carefully chopped off and laid in a tray. The blood, however, started to boil and bubble over, and a new sacrifice was needed to restore harmony. At this point the story becomes muddled; several mythical strands are intertwined, and what emerges is a second sacrifice – of the prophet or of his father, who is sawn in two from head to foot (and even from shoulder to shoulder), thereby merging with the icon of the Cosmic Man sacrificed at the beginning of time, of the Primal Androgyne whose sacrifice gives birth to the present world, as that of St John inaugurates the new dispensation (see Bausani 1964). It appears that the sawing in two motif was interpreted by Ismaili esoteric circles in the sense of Kundalini-raising yogic practices leading to an androgynous consciousness (see Ummul Kitab 1966).

As usual, the Hindu parallels are numerous and enlightening.

The sage Caitanya went into deep meditation and was covered by an anthill, only his eyes showing through two holes (like the sun in the cavern of the autumn equinox). The king's daughter pierced them, out of curiosity, and the kingdom was threatened with drought. The princess remedied the situation by marrying the sage. Later, her chastity having first been proved, the sage's eyesight and youth was restored to him by the Divine Twins, just as the sun is revived at the spring equinox.

Another myth (see Schulman 1977) recounts that a goddess hid in an anthill. The king unknowingly started hacking away at it with an axe, and when he saw that he had wounded the goddess, he tore out his own bowels and offered them to her for food. She then allowed him stay with her. Her priest dresses as a woman.

The Deity-in-the-anthill seems to be male to the female and female to the male. The anthill is considered the androgyne axis of nature not only in southern India, but in Africa and Australia, the home of Rainbowsnake (see also p. 57).

The myth comes out most clearly in the version of the cycle of Indra, the sky-god. One day he was robbed of the divine intoxicant or moon-juice, *soma*, by Namuci, who was unassailable with weapons wrought of the four elements, and could not be attacked either during the day or at night. Indra therefore forged a *vajra*, or *lingam*, out of foam, which is neither water nor air, and attacked the thief at twilight. With the *vajra* he bisected Namuci into male and female.

The head was the male section, and it started rolling after Indra, reproaching him – the god could free himself of its persecution only by washing his hands at the confluence of two rivers (see also pp. 86–87).

Another Indra myth tells of him having to drink *soma* from the mouth of the horrible seeress Apāla, who enjoins him to 'replant' her father's head in a field and to 'replant' her barren womb.

The motifs in the myths of the severed head (of the androgyne) are:

a) There is a cosmic cavern or tree or anthill.

b) Inside it is concealed the androgyne, the Primal God, or the God who assumes the opposite sex to that of the worshipper.

c) An act of violence or of love blinds, bisects or beheads the androgyne.

d) The severed head or the lost eyesight becomes a cause of trouble; a sacrifice has to be made.

e) Balance is restored, the androgyne made whole once more, *soma* restored to its owner, and the land healed.

All these symbols happen to be neatly explained in the Buddhist treatise Vanmīka Sutta. The anthill (a) is the body; the 'indwelling cobra' (b) is the adept; the 'fire' or 'eyes' are his actions, and the 'pick-axe' is the insight he develops (c). It is the sword of Gnosis that severs the head of the Baptist and uses it as a eucharist, to absorb the androgyne wisdom (see pp. 84–85).

Early Christianity

St John the Baptist taught a ritual of baptism that coincides with the usual plunge of the androgyne (see pp. 86–87). The baptized would put on the garment of glory – the image of God stamped on Adam the Androgyne, on the Adam of Light, from whose phallus flow the waters of life.

Mandaean priests, the inheritors of the original teaching of the Baptist, ritually pronounce the cup of consecrated wine to be the cosmic womb, and declare that the original Adam is reconstituted in it (see Drower 1960).

This imagery and its meaning were taken on by the Christian community. In Galatians 3:28 St Paul states that after baptism there is no longer a distinction between male and female. (The image of the flow of living waters from the belly of 'he that believeth', John 7:38, also harks back to the Mandaean one of the Adam of Light.)

Gnostic circles delved deeper into androgyny. Besides baptism, a series of Gnostic sacraments (see Robinson 1977) were supposed to clothe man in 'the image of God', restoring his androgyny. The peak was reached with the 'Chrism in the Bridal Chamber', (the act of anointing) which was supposed to recreate the 'communion' of Jesus with Mary Magdalen. What actually took place remains unknown – it was supposed to be a celebration of the hierogamy of 'before the foundation of the world' and thereby an 'iconization' of the participants. It implied that shame was transcended and childish innocence restored, that the inside was made as the outside, the above as the below, the female (inner) as the male (outer). The fully initiated became a *monachos*, a dweller in plenitude.

In *The Little Interrogation of Mary* of the Nag Hammadi library, a crude enactment of the creation of Eve as described in Genesis is ascribed to Jesus himself: He takes a disciple called Mary to the top of a mountain and there appears to extract a woman from his side, and to make love to her. Mary faints. When she revives she is told that if she cannot bear disclosures in earthly terms, much less would she be able to stand spiritual revelations.

According to Hippolytus, the Gnostics addressed prayers to the same 'persons' as the Qabbalistic texts read into 'IHVH': 'From the Father and through Thee, Mother, you two immortal Names, Parents of the divine being and you in heaven, humanity of the powerful name ...' Marcos taught his followers to discern in the wine the blood of the Mother and to pray that 'She who is before all things, incomprehensible and indescribable Grace, fill within, increasing her knowledge within'. In the Gnostic text *The Great Announcement*, the two 'sides' of God, male and female, are addressed.

The Naassenes, or 'Worshippers of the Serpent', who were followers of Jesus' brother James, adopted the double axe as a symbol for the eternal androgyne nature in man which they sought to restore. In Samaritan Naassene circles, enlightenment was attained through the ritual worship of a serpent and the eating of hallucinogenic eucharistic bread made from the mandragora mushroom (see Bagatti 1973). Among Judaeo-Christians the double axe denoted androgyny, and the cross-as-tree-of-life and the trefoil symbolized the *lingam*, just as the fish and the horns symbolized the *yoni*. Their fusion was emphasized in the inscriptions on the walls of their initiation chambers in cemeteries (see Testa 1962).

Ritual castration was also sometimes performed among early Christians (by Origen, for example) 'for the Kingdom' – a custom revived even in modern times by the Russian *skopcy*.

After the initial (mostly Gnostic) theoretical stress on the subject, discussions of androgyny were progressively forced out of the mainstream of ecclesiastical thought. In the period from St Paul to St Augustine the disclosures of esoteric lore that had marked early Christianity were silenced one by one. The very idea of divine nothingness was limited to the Dionysian tradition. The mystical transcendence of ethical dichotomies was not insisted upon. The innocent, loving, shared life of spiritual men and women devoted to prayer that is depicted in the *Pastor of Hermas* was condemned by the Church, as a danger to chastity, in its fulminations against *virgines subintroductae*, the insinuated virgins. Later, in newly converted Ireland, the same way of life took root in monasteries and was called *consortium mulierum* (fellowship of women). In the *Comrac Liadaine Ocus Chuirithir* the story is told of a poet and a poetess who under the guidance of St Cummine first converse but do not look upon each other, and later sleep together with a child between them, but finally have to separate.

The particular experience of spiritual elation that flares up between mystics of opposite sexes could never be totally proscribed by ecclesiastical suspicion, and it surfaces all through the history of Christianity. St Francis and St Claire, St Theresa and St John of the Cross, St François de Sales and Ste Jeanne-Françoise de Chantal, Fénelon and Madame de Guyon are the most famous cases in which mystical transcendence is intensified by the peculiar vortex of spiritual energies that leads to the formation of an androgyne subtle psychic being.

Mystics and theologians such as the ninth-century Scotus Erigena who soared beyond the limits of a personal and male concept of the godhead, and felt and restated the presence of the archetype of androgyny, risked the ban of the Church. Their ideas went underground, and the parallel Jewish esoteric culture became the store-house into which daring, searching souls dipped for knowledge through the centuries. Along with Jewish esotericism,

The alchemical process of fusion through fermentation – here represented by a king and a queen lying side by side, their souls hovering above their naked bodies – shares the aim of early Christian ascetic couples: to liberate the animating principles through fermentation and fusion of the subtle bodies. (From Daniel Stolchius, Viridarium chymicum, *Frankfurt, 1624.)*

A reminiscence of the bearded Venuses of Greek cults and of the androgyne Christ, the icon of a bearded girl on a cross finds its supporting legend in the martyrdom of St Wilgefortis (or St Kümmernis), a Christian girl who miraculously developed a beard to save herself from the assault of her heathen persecutor. The saint is here associated with learning (the book) and with the reconciliation of duality (the T-shaped cross).

there was also the Hermetic tradition, whose doctrine of androgyny was summed up in a famous passage of *Asclepius*: ' "Then you say, Trismegistus, that God is both sexes?" – "Yes, and not only God, Asclepius, but all things animate and inanimate, for both sexes teem with reproductive power, and their binding power, or rather unity, which you call Venus or Cupid or both is beyond understanding – highest charity, joy, mirth, desire, and divine love are innate in it".'

The Church was able to avoid an overt treatment of androgyny because of its psychological balancing of the male severity of the Father and the female intercession of the Virgin, with the Son to hold the balance. Melville in the chapter called 'The Tail' in *Moby Dick* caught the psychological message of the Son, as He was propounded by Catholic iconology: 'the "soft, curled, hermaphroditical" Italian pictures, so destitute of all brawnishness, hint nothing of any power, but the mere negative, feminine one of submission and endurance.' Seen in this light, the circumcision of Jesus, on which such stress was laid iconologically, and hence archetypally, takes on its full significance as token emasculation.

In the school of Chartres, too, the idea of divine androgyny was cultivated. Alanus ab Insulis visualized the divine Intellect as the dwelling-place of all seeds, whose womb is nature. On the heretic fringe of the medieval Church, Abelard even voiced the Rabbinic idea that God's image is the maleness of the soul – and his likeness its femaleness.

The androgyne myth of Narcissus who drowned in a pool (see p. 20) was preserved in the 'epigram of the hermaphrodite' (see Jung 1970) which was written down by Mathieu de Vendôme as early as about 1150. A pregnant woman is promised a boy by Apollo, a girl by Mars, and by Juno neither one nor the other; to this enigmatic offspring Apollo promises death by water, Mars death on the cross, and Juno death by a weapon. The hermaphrodite, the epigram concludes, climbed a tree overhanging water, his-her sword slipped and struck him-her. He-she was caught on a branch and his-her head dangled in the water.

In other variants the hermaphrodite, the indefinable being, is called Aelia Laelia Crispis, and is neither man, nor woman, nor androgyne, neither a child nor a youth, nor an old person, neither chaste, nor a whore, but everything.

A legend about the great fourteenth-century German mystic Meister Eckhart relates that one day a girl announced herself at his monastery gate as his daughter, as having no name, as being neither a virgin nor a spouse nor a widow, neither a lord nor a lady, neither a thrall nor a wench. The mystic wanted to know more, so his 'daughter' explained that she was all of these things, and their opposites, in relation to God. In the light of this legend, Aelia Laelia Crispis would seem to be the spiritual offspring, the transcendent new identity of a mystic soul. In 1567 Richard White of Basingstoke explained the riddle as follows: Aelia Laelia Crispis is the soul, which is male in women, female in men. Aelia is solar, Laelia lunar, Crispis earthly. When the soul acquires knowledge of herself, she discerns her source lying above duality, in divine wisdom. Thus, in the words of an apparently nonsensical riddle, metaphysicians through the centuries were able to give voice to what Śivaite devotees of Ardhanārīśvara Śiva, the

Androgyne Lord, went through the streets of India freely singing, praising Him who is neither god nor demon, neither mortal nor animal, not a Brahmin, neither man nor woman nor eunuch.

> ...the self that hovers
> in between
> is neither man
> nor woman.

(Speaking of Śiva, trs. A. K. Ramanujan, London 1973.)

Androgyny and power in Christianity

The idea of androgyny persisted tacitly in the sphere of politics. Empire is a blending of severity and mercy, mercy compensating for severity in an androgyne balance of forces. The tradition of the hermaphrodite ruler goes back to Assyria. When Roman emperors sought to strengthen their ideological hold on peoples where the cult of the androgyne was strong, they had recourse to androgynous myths and initiations.

Roman history was written by partisans of the political philosophy that considered the Empire to be a kind of lease to the ruler from 'The Roman people and Senate', so almost everything that we know of the emperors who sought to justify their power on other grounds takes the form of slanderous and far-fetched tales.

Caligula, Nero, Commodus and Heliogabalus (Marcus Aurelius Antoninus) established their rule on religious doctrines based on the androgyne character of supreme authority, so they all come in for punishment at the hands of the historians or of satirists like Juvenal, who pretend to take the mystical metaphor of their betrothals to the gods literally, attributing to them the homosexual marriages, the incests, the transvestism of the Roman riff-raff (see Colin 1956).

It is possible that in the case of Heliogabalus (204–22 AD), the wild soldiery were mesmerized by the dancing boy – Emperor's display of bisexual charm. Told by Couperus, the early twentieth-century Dutch novelist in his *Heliogabalus,* the scene seems convincing.

With the adoption of Christianity, the Roman emperors acquired an apparently solid archetypal standing, as 'icons of Christ'. Since in Byzantium the emperor was also the chief authority in ecclesiastical matters, he represented the supreme couple, Christ and his Church.

There are bisexual elements in the Imperial ceremonies and in the very implication of the emperor as 'restorer of Eden' and 'Messiah', as he was now called.

He was surrounded by candelabra representing the Tree of Life as a burning bush (fire being male) and he sat on the throne, the matrix of kingship. He was the male spear-bearer and measurer of time, but also the female wearer of the crown and measurer of the sacred space of the city. He represented both male victory and female peace (see Miller 1971).

When Byzantium started to lose its hold on central Italy, the Church of Rome sought to extricate its ecclesiastical authority from Imperial power, and the frescoes in the Roman basilica of SS. Quattuor Coronati depict the consequent political philosophy – Constantine was seen as a leprous sovereign, like a wounded Grail fisher-king in need of renewal. He was healed by baptism, and in thanks, as though in payment, he symbolically held the reins of the Pope's white horse. The motherly quality of empire was vested in the Pope, who ritually gave birth to the Church during the coronation ceremony at the Lateran basilica (see p. 40). He would sit sprawled out on a midwife's chair, which is preserved to this day (see D'Onofrio 1979). The rite died out when the Vatican chapter grew powerful at the expense of the Lateran. The canons of the Vatican then created the legend of Joan, the English girl who, masquerading as a man, studied in Byzantium, and succeeded in being nominated Pope, but on her way to be crowned in the Lateran unfortunately gave birth to a child.

In the Western Empire, Imperial femaleness was assumed by the Church, which also took on, in part at least, its inseparable maleness. The Roman Christian Empire in the West never recovered from this lack of inherent imperial androgyny. In the East, however, the Byzantine Empire, whose symbol was the double eagle, persisted in its archetypal duality up to that watershed of history, 1453, when Byzantium fell to the Turks.

Abiding power is always androgyne. The ruler must always appear poor as well as rich, needy as well as lavish. He must show a vulnerable, suffering, even persecuted part of himself. The appeal of the truly powerful must be not only to inspire fear and wonder, but also pity and even contempt. Mesopotamian kings were slapped in the face and supposed to weep at coronations. The image of the most lasting institution in the West, the Catholic Church, comprised magnificence, splendour, overbearing majesty and pitiful beggary. The scarlet pomp of the Cardinal and the monk's tattered rags, the strong fist of the Swiss guard and the soothing fingers of the sister of charity, were, if not the two heads of the double eagle of empire, the two keys to the human heart.

A strong ruler must be all-seeing and at the same time easily deceived. There must be an ideal state and an actual state management apparently at loggerheads. The state must be both the Heavenly Lady and the stern ruthless ruler. One must be able to appeal to her against him, and vice versa if one is shocked by too much leniency.

A ruler must always be able somehow to connect with the seething opposition to his government. He must even create it. He must never allow anything *opposite* to subsist totally outside his influence. He shall always bear in mind that nothing can subsist without a counterpart, so no sooner does he entrust power to a minister than he must leak some help to that minister's rival. (No sooner were the Jesuits well established at the Chinese court, than they helped arm and strengthen the Barbarian armies on the border. They took the risk because only by becoming the pivot of balance could they hope to last.)

A political body which aims at universality must be able to envisage all possible activities together with their counter-activities. The education it gives its members is simply a cultivation of what they already are – they follow their innate calling and the androgyne power provides work for them, just as it does for their rivals. All it needs to do is tip the scales now and then, when the need is felt. By fighting one another, enemies serve the power that holds the balance between them.

All systems of political checks and balances are intrinsically androgyne.

After the Reformation

With the stamping out of Catholicism in England, people started dreaming of the repressed androgyne. The spirit of the Reformation opened the way for a revival of this whole hidden strain in Christian thought. The Catholic Church practised androgyny in its politics, but refrained from acknowledging it theologically, whereas Protestants, who were purely male-minded politicians, opened up to androgyny in a spiritual way.

Spenser, who forged his epic poem, *The Faerie Queen*, in the service of an ideal of Protestant chivalry, used the image of the hermaphrodite to convey the idea of a complete blending of two souls (III, XII; see also pp. 72–73).

> *No word they spake, no earthly thing they felt*
> *But like two senceless stocks in long embracement dwelt.*

The two souls have reached the condition of the highest power in the universe – that of 'the [great goddesse] great dame Nature, whose port is goodly', who 'is gracious in majesty',

> *Yet certes by her face and physnomy*
> *Whether she man or woman inly were,*
> *That could not any creature weel descry.*

She is hidden behind a veil, either to conceal her terrifying lion-like face or to dim her splendour, of which the sun is only a reflected image. Spenser compares her substance to that of the transfigured bodies on Mount Tabor. She is the eternally young grandmother of all creatures, moving and unmoved, unseen of any, by all beheld – knitting all her creatures in a brotherly bond. Her androgyne perfection is above mutability. She forms the seeds of all species, and their nature is confirmed through all changes. They rule therefore over mutability, and are what the ancients called Adonis or Attis, the Ever-Dying and Ever-Resurrected, unceasingly stamping matter with the forms of undying species.

With the new atmosphere of Protestant mysticism the archetype started becoming apparent to many, while the only Catholic to be obsessed with androgyny, Guillaume Postel, was doomed to fall out of the ranks. He dreamed of a return to Adamic plenitude, in which the female, physical aspect of creation would be transformed by a woman Christ, whom he thought he had actually met in Venice, a matron serving the suffering in a hospital, the scoff of everyone. To him she was the *Anima mundi*, the world-soul which encompassed within it Christ, the *Animus mundi* or world-spirit. Postel felt that he himself was their first-born androgyne, clothed in the two vestments of glory, the red (female) and the white (male) seed. (The bibliography and manuscript sources are examined in Pittaluga 1979.)

In seventeenth-century Germany a new kind of Protestant mysticism flourished, which was based on the cult of androgyne Adam. Jacob Behmen enjoyed visions of Adam (see p. 43), and his disciples went back to the primitive Christian notions of androgyny.

Johann G. Gichtel, the foremost of Behmen's followers, taught that earthly maleness and femaleness must be discarded in order to achieve unity with the Father and with his Presence Sophia, the tincture of Light (see also p. 60). Sophia, he believed, had been the helpmeet of Adam's fiery soul, but Adam was attracted to the animals and to the greater duality implied in their relative imperfection, and was henceforth sundered from her. She, the light, found a new husband of fire in Jesus, whom she received in her womb. And if, as Gichtel recommends, we place her in our imagination, she will give birth to Jesus within us. She is God's *Fiat* (power of creation); if we blend with her we shall have the power of *Fiat* in our mouth, her virginal fortitude in our heart.

Antoinette Bourignon was born in Lille in 1616, a Catholic, but her visionary spirit brought her into the maincurrent of Behmenite mysticism (see Bourignon 1679–86 and Hutin 1960). She had a vision of Adam's belly with a vessel in it, in which small eggs germinated, and another vessel full of a liquid that fecundated them. When Adam as the first human was fired with love for God and with the desire to see him worshipped by more and more souls, the liquid was blissfully spilt from one vessel to the next and the eggs dropped out, developing into living, worshipping beings. After the resurrection this shall be the way of the glorified flesh of all men.

John Pordage, head of the Philadelphians, a seventeenth-century English sect, taught that Sophia is the female part or side of Adam. By uniting with her, Pordage hoped to become one with the transfigured Christ. He consorted with Jane Lead, a poor London widow, who in 1676 beheld a vision of Sophia dressed in a transparent golden apparel, with a sun-like countenance. From the vision, she learnt that the Virgin Mary had been but a type of Sophia.

In William Blake's mind the archetype acted so strongly that a brand new mythology developed, in which the remaining Christian terms were charged with fresh meaning. God, or Eternal Man, he taught, was originally androgyne beyond female space and male time, but he fell from that perfection, expelling from his completeness a series of projections, starting with Albion, 'a Shadow from his weary intellect'. Albion is reminiscent of the Behmenite conception of Adam. In one vision he is seen fighting Luvah (the earth, love or the morning of the cosmos), turning her ears outwards, bending her nostrils down, enveloping in fear her 'fluxile eyes' and shrinking up her lips and tongue. This is the phase which in traditional metaphysics corresponds to the contraction of non-manifest reality to possible forms. Blake did not stick to one visionary version of this phase. He also pictured it as a separation of Eternal Man into two parts, and put these lines in the mouth of the splitting creature:

In Blake's Spirit of Fire, *the archetype of the Androgyne of Fire comes to life, the impersonation of primal matter about to send forth the specific forms of nature. (Line engraving with some etching, from* For the Sexes: The Gates of Paradise, *London, 1793.)*

Blind in Fire with shield & spear,
Two Horn'd Reasoning, Cloven Fiction,
In Doubt, which is Self contradiction,
A dark Hermaphrodite We stood,
Rational Truth, Root of Evil & Good,
Round me flew the Flaming Sword;
Round her snowt Whirlwinds roar'd,
Freezing her Veil, the Mundane Shell

(The Gates of Paradise, in *The Poetry and Prose of William Blake*, ed. G. Keynes, London 1948.)

The world of names and forms follows (see pp. 66–67), in which man as the hard reasoner and conqueror, Urizen, will see his female counterpart in dreams as a mournful vision, as a watery spectre of moist locks, reflecting all his indolence, his weakness, his wish for death.

The complexities of Blake's vision are still to a vast extent a sealed treasure, yet many feel that in his dark words there lies a revelation capable of helping the human race out of its present-day plight. We suffer for the loss of all the female qualities in us – the art of listening to forewarnings, of accepting frailty, of feeling tenderness toward the cosmos. Masculine regimentation, planning, utilitarian exploitation have grown to the extent of bringing us to the verge of self-destruction. From childhood we are tortured into assuming that the left side of the brain is our only worthy guide. The last nooks in the world where spiritual delicacy used to be allowed to influence life have been cleared out and laid open to Urizen's ruthlessness.

Blake's indictment of the Fall seems to speak of the core of our predicament:

The Feminine separates from the Masculine & both from Man,
Ceasing to be His Emanations, Life to Themselves assuming.

(Jerusalem, IV, 90, in *The Poetry and Prose of William Blake*, ed. G. Keynes, London 1948.)

The androgyne now seems once more to be astir. Perhaps it will make ears bend to Melville's

The innocent if lawless elf,
Ethereal in virginity
Though yielding easy rein indeed,
To impulse which the fibers breed.
. . . .

Such natures, and but such, have got
Familiar with strange things that dwell
Repressed in mortals

(Clarel. A Poem and Pilgrimage to the Holy Land, New York 1960.)

Avalokiteśvara, the Buddha of our cycle of time (see also p. 37), is known in Kashmir as Matsyendranath, the fisher and the fish. His usual icon shows him in the act of bursting into eleven heads, out of compassion for the sufferings of all sentient beings. Simple Buddhist devotees seek consolation from him, who is the fountainhead of all love. Practitioners go beyond this phase of mere faith, and visualize him to the point of hallucination. They live in his presence, receiving his love, soothed and mellowed by his understanding and forgiveness. At this point he can become, as in the experience of Chinese adepts, the Lady of Mercy.

At the final stage, the adept realizes that Avalokiteśvara, with all his-her power of compassion, is nothing but a projection of the mind, and liberation is achieved, beyond forms and words.

In Hinduism the role of Avalokiteśvara belongs to Śiva, who at Maturai becomes a sow to nurse some orphaned piglets, and is worshipped as Śiva Mātṛbhūteśvara ('Śiva who became a mother'). In Assam he transforms himself into a buffalo cow.

Malekulan rituals (see Layard 1977) enable us to understand the esoteric use of assuming a motherly form. Malekulan initiations entail the performance of one's own funeral rites and then giving birth to oneself as 'Lord Mother'. He-she is then unified once more as 'Mother-with-Child', and exerts authority in the Mother's name, as her executive and spokesman. (Avalokiteśvara, silver statue, India, 20th c.)

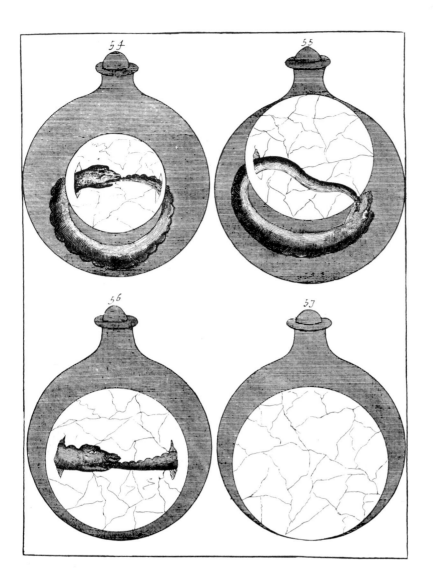

The phase of yellowing (*citrinitas*) of the alchemical primal matter, or Philosophic Egg (left), and a regulus of antimony show how alchemists interpreted the latent workings of nature. Regulus is the purified metal that, on reduction, remains at the bottom of the crucible; the star regulus of antimony is known for its readiness to combine with gold; its structure is repeated in the alchemical drawing, but here the movements of a snake depict the spirit of gold, which animates the regulus on a subtle level.

The regulus ('little king') of antimony can take the form of a star, recalling the star Regulus, the heart of the constellation of Leo, the Lion. Is it then the lion, the king of metals?

Isaac Newton worked on regulus antimony, confident that it contained a strong sulphurous principle, or Philosophical Sulphur. He mixed it with silver, and out came a lead mass, which he surmised might be an androgyne first matter (see also pp. 42–43, 66, 78). This he mixed with mercury, confident that this might attract Mercurius, the free-floating spirit of transmutations, from the air (see also pp. 76–77).

He carried out all the cryptic advice of the texts: 'You shall pass through iron!'; and 'iron was in the original ore'; 'You shall use a magnet!' Just one cup of antimony can be used to prepare medicine by pouring water into it, indefinitely, so strongly does it, like a magnet, impregnate the free-floating, enlivening influences of the air. 'You shall use lead!': a Philosophical Lead was created.

When Newton finally mixed his preparation with gold, he saw trees branching out in the sealed jars on the fire, appearing and disappearing, and a rainbow of changing colours, seen here as the serpentine rotating movements in the alchemical drawing.

B. J. T. Dobbs (1975) offers the explanation that 'unstable inter-metallic compounds' flashed out under Newton's eyes. Alchemists would have said that he had washed the Androgyne of Fire, which had responded flashing its 'rainbow' or 'Peacock's Tail'. (The Yellowing of the Primal Matter, drawing from Johann Conrad Barchusen, *Elementa Chemiae*, Leiden, 1718.)

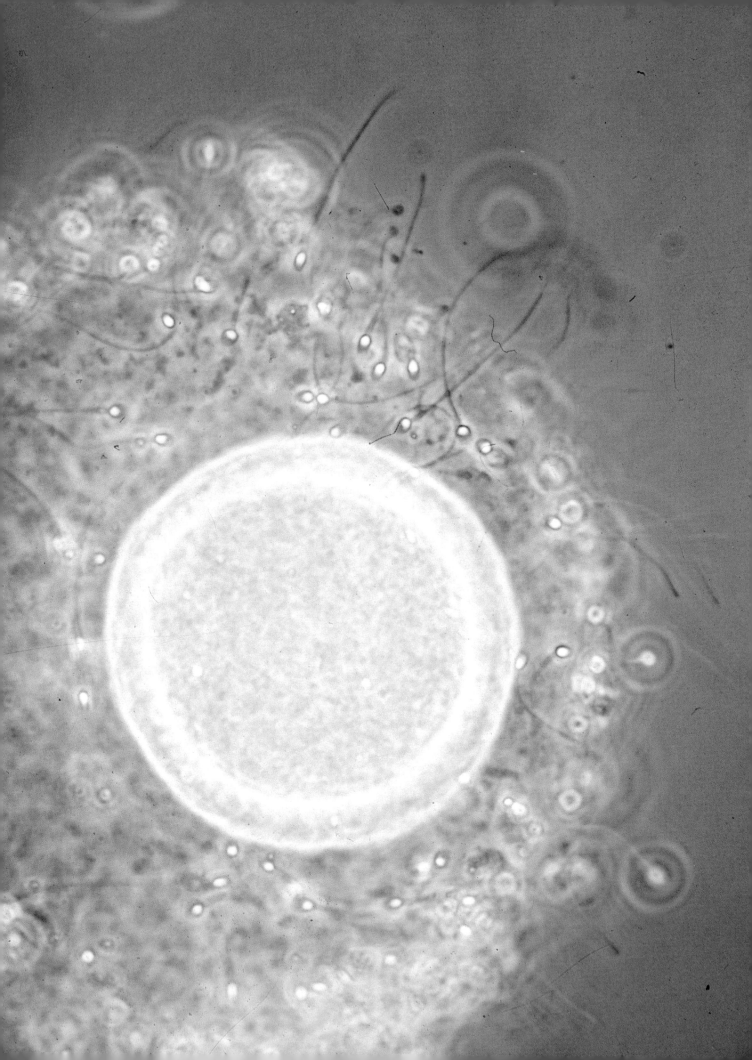

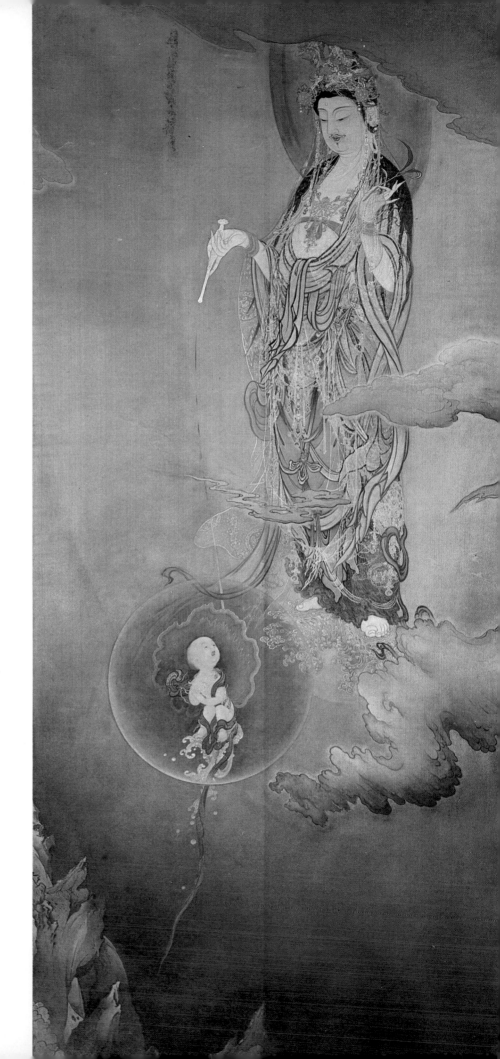

Male sperm forms a circle enclosing the ovum, which one sperm will eventually penetrate and dissolve, forming what alchemists would have called the androgyne living primal matter, which was thought to persist in its androgyny until the foetus is limited to a specific sex. The interpenetration of what corresponds to sperm and ovum in the field of metals was represented by the serpent biting its tail (see p. 34).

Moustached Kannon (the Chinese Kuan Yin, see p. 33) pours the spirit of life (or the dew of compassion) from her vase into the child's body. The vase is the same as Avalokiteśvara's, and sometimes has a spout in the shape of the *garuda*, the messenger bird of the Indian gods. Its symbolism is the same as that of the red lotus or the willow branch, which are also sometimes placed in Kannon's hand. On an esoteric level they are all connected with inspiration through dreams: the most precious form of the spirit of life and dew of compassion. (Hibbo Kannon by Kano Hogai, colour on silk, Japan, 19th c.)

The woodcut shows the word or the waters of life flowing from the Ineffable – from supraformal reality – and becoming the word as such, the Son, who divides the sleeping androgyne. In Vedanta, woman arises in the void left by a contraction of the Supreme Identity. This absolute (*Atman*) was, according to the *Bṛhadaranyaka Upaniṣad* (I, iv, 1–3) alone as a person, an 'I-am' identity similar to a man and a woman conjoined. He-she produced a void (*akaṣa*, sheer space) and it was filled by woman. Modern science, on the other hand, sees maleness as the result of an imposition of male characteristics on the foetus. (Four-month foetus in the amniotic sac; woodcut from the Cologne Bible, Germany, 15th c.)

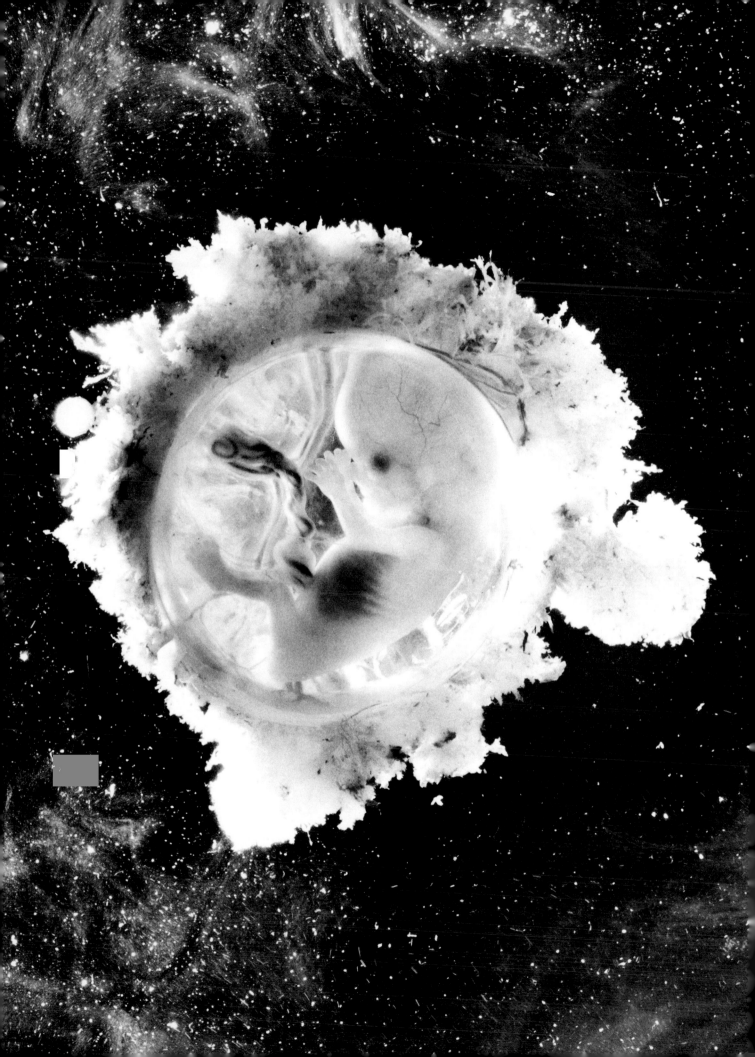

The legend of Pope Joan, who gave birth to a child before her papal coronation ceremony, originated from a peculiar ritual, a sacred pantomime in the Lateran, in which the Pope as androgyne gave birth to the Church (see also p. 28).

The Pope represented the New Adam, whose bride was the Church, as Israel had been the bride of the One Lord. But the New Adam was also supposed to give birth to his Church, to whom he was both father-mother and husband. The world of divine life is a world of androgyne perfection. (Pope Joan Giving Birth, ms. illustration from Ms. 5193, f.371, France, 15th c.)

Adam was plunged into a swoon (compare the myth of Narcissus, the Swooner, on p. 20), and the first fall took place with the loss of androgyny. In Christian symbolism the extraction of Eve from Adam's side is usually shown as the work of God the Son, of the Word which is the discerner of hearts, the principle of division itself, 'sharper than any two-edged sword, piercing even to the dividing asunder of soul and spirit, and of the joints and marrow' (Hebrews 4:12). Eve was interpreted as the soul, the life of the senses, and a now diminished Adam as will and reason, the spirit. The only remaining link between them after

the fall was imagination. They would imagine each other as their respective needs, so in order to tempt them to their second fall, Satan became a serpent, which St Augustine interpreted as imagination incarnate. To redress all this, the Son or Word was said to have entered into the womb of a daughter of Eve (whom he had originally extracted from Adam's side), in order to be born of her as a New Adam, a 'First-Engendered', yet born of woman. The womanliness in man could now participate in the mystery of God's incarnation through identification with the model for womanhood, who was daughter of her son, mother of her father and virgin wife of both. All family ties, the strongest, or at least most stable, emotional forces in man, were evoked and trebled, made bewildering by paradox and associated with these basic theological conceptions. This kind of 'divine' family romance was concocted by ecclesiastical institutions to secure strong emotional appeal. However, imagining oneself living through it led to the inner restoration of the emotional and rational completeness of, and total participation in, lost androgyny. (The Creation of Eve, fresco by Bartolo di Fredi, Italy, 14th c.)

Albert the Great, Thomas Aquinas'
master, points at an androgyne
holding a Y. Albert, the text informs
us, here represents supreme authority, both spiritual and temporal.
The Y is, as Philo taught, the symbol
of the Word which pierces the
essence of beings. The Naassene
Gnostics taught that it represented
the intimate nature of being, which
is male and female and, as such,
eternal. (Albertus Magnus, engraving from Michael Maier, *Symbola
aureae mensae*, Frankfurt 1617.)

This was the basic teaching of
alchemy, which is expounded symbolically in Khunrath's globe. The
centre and essence of the earth is
Chaos, which is shown as an androgyne (Rebis), who combines
contraction and expansion, female

and male, into a unified spiral; this is the creative force in reality. The two opposites are engaged and put into gear by the essence of light which takes the form of Saltiness, of a burning acridity in the bowels of the earth. The spiral of the activated androgyne produces the 'Peacock's Tail' or 'Rainbow': matter quickened and energized, about to produce the seed of mineral and vegetable bodies. (Androgyny in the Primal State of Chaos, engraving from Henricus Khunrath, *Amphitheatrum sapientiae*, Antwerp 1609.)

The practical application of the theory is hinted at in the androgyne on the fire. Androgyne primal matter, in the mineral world, lies in a state of latency, under an eclipsed sun and a new moon. In order to quicken and grow, to receive the invisible rays from the sun and the moon, and to develop into a mineral seed, the androgyne needs the fire of fermentation. This is the general teaching. In the actual preparation of alchemical medicines this means that two opposite substances, such as mercury and sulphur, should be imbued with certain juices and then ground to a fine black powder. This powder is placed in a sealed vase and kept at a low heat until it ferments. The joined bodies in the engraving symbolize the powdered substances, the surrounding darkness the sealed vase, the grilling the special 'heat of fermentation' necessary for bringing off the transformation. This process can be seen even today in any Indian factory of ayurvedic drugs.

Workmen chip the vase periodically to inspect the degree of transformation – indicated by changes in colour – of the substances. This phase is symbolized in Western texts by the Peacock's Tail rising above the androgyne.

To a mystic, what goes on in the closed vase is genesis on a small scale. The process was visualized by Jacob Behmen in *Von der Gnadenwahl* (1623): 'Adam clad in utmost Glory, neither man nor woman, but both, with both tinctures tempered both as Heavenly Matrix, in the procreative fire of Love, and as Maleness akin to the essential fire' (5:35). (Androgyne on the Fire, engraving from Michael Maier, *Atalanta fugiens*, Frankfurt 1617.)

The myth of Hermaphroditus is relived in Magritte's painting, which also recalls one of Freud's patients: attempting to explain the episode that had triggered her symptoms, she enacted a rape scene, one hand pulling her skirt down, the other ripping it off. There is an underlying unity between the shy nymph (reluctant femininity) and lusty Pan (forceful virility). The blushing of the nymph offers a mirror to Pan's longing, and vice versa. The two opposing forces of reluctance and aggressiveness revolve on a common pivot. This same fusion is the reason for the slightly disturbing challenge of Andrew Logan's costume, which zigzags like a streak of lightning, tracing the median line between the two sexes, while the wearer fixes the onlooker with a cold, narcissistic gaze. (Gigantic Days, oil painting by René Magritte, France, 20th c.)

This mask was used as a helmet; the black face is its male aspect, the white its female. Naturally the Ezagham people are reticent when enquiries are made as to its meaning, and tend to put you off with answers such as 'it denotes heaven and earth', or 'night and day', or 'the knowledge of past and future'; or else they tell the story of a married couple who lost all their relatives, so had to defend themselves on their own, with two guns – the husband firing and the wife recharging – and thus overcame all their enemies. A simple story, but also a perfect parable of the androgyne nature of power, usually typified by the double eagle (see p. 28). (Wooden mask, Nigeria.)

Androgyne primal matter on an urn, whose four sections represent the four elements. The wings denote its incipient volatility due to the engaging of its solar, centripetal and its lunar, centrifugal energies (the king and queen) which spiral into a process of fermentation. To add up the symbolism of the drawing: the interpenetrating solar ○ and lunar ☽ principles upon the cross made by the elements + together make up the sign of Mercurius ☿ with the wings of volatility jutting upwards. (Alchemical androgyne, from Arnold of Villanova, *Rosarium philosophorum*, Ms. 394a, 16th c. Stadtbibliothek Vadiana, St Gallen.)

Unity: birth and the serpent

William Blake expressed a widespread tradition, especially alive with the al-chemists, in assuming that visible matter is preceded by an invisible fermentation in which the male principle of light and time, like a 'flaming sword' starts rotating within the veil of ice and snow of the female principle, which is the essence of space (see p. 31). The frozen veil or solid shell of the female aspect of primal matter forms the visible appearance of reality: of cosmic delusion, or *māyā*. All this can be pictured in terms of an egg, in which male sun or time (which is but the sun's shadow upon dials) is repre-sented by the yolk, and female space by the albumen and the visible shell. In the alchemical drawing the egg becomes the globe, its albumen the pap of vege-tation, its yolk the sun, here represented as the male head of the androgyne whose female feet stand in the element of water at the bottom of the valley or womb placed between the two hills of

fire (the salamander) and air (the eagles). Cosmic Man appears as the child, the replica of the androgyne globe.

In Blake's engraving (from *The Gates of Paradise*) Cosmic or Eternal Man is seen as a winged Eros breaking through the shell. This echoes the Greek tradi-tion of Eros as the god of the origin of life. Blake places in his mouth the lines

I rent the Veil where the Dead dwell:
When weary Man enters his Cave
He meets his Savior in the Grave.
Some find a Female Garment there,
And some a Male, woven with care.

(*For Children: The Gates of Paradise*, in *The Poetry and Prose of William Blake*, ed. G. Keynes, London 1948.)

Eternal Man is the rapturous awareness of being, prior to all sense of space and time, the limitless and infinite essence of all life. His fall begins when he is trapped in the egg of the 'dead'. Breaking out of it, he finds himself in the Cave of Deceit, the world of 'local habitations', of names and forms. Here his Saviour (from deceit) is the Worm of Death, which weaves for

him garments of flesh and blood, which are either male or female. The same idea is implied in the Tantric painting left: from the yolk and the white of the egg develop, respectively, red (male) or white (female) dots in space and time. Blake says that when Eternal Man dons his mortal, sexed garment, it conceals from him his true, eternal self. The Tantric painting separates with a frame the world of the egg from the world of sexed individuals. The garments, Blake says, can be 'sweet'; they can give access to timeless and spaceless ecstasy, which he calls 'exuberance'. In exuberance, eternal Man is resurrected, and in resurrection he may 'change his garment at will'.

The hatching of the egg is depicted as the work of a serpent, possibly a double serpent (below left), coiling round the egg (opposite top left, below right). As Rainbowsnake (below left) it manifests itself in all creative changes in nature and can be written in symbolical shorthand as concentric circles expanding from a centre (see also pp. 14, 57).

Left-hand page:
Kundalini coiled around an egg-lingam. Stone, India, 20th c. Collection Ajit Mookerjee.

'At length for hatching ripe/He breaks the shell'. Line engraving by William Blake from *For Children: The Gates of Paradise*, London, 1793. British Library, London.

The separation of individual forms from the primal unity. Gouache on paper, India, 18th c. Collection Ajit Mookerjee.

Right-hand page:
Alchemical androgyne. From J. D. Mylius, *Philosophia reformata*, Frankfurt, 1622.

Aranda *churinga*. Australia, aboriginal. Museum of Mankind, London.

The snake of the Marinbata people, Arnhemland. Australia, aboriginal.

Five-hooded serpent and egg-lingam. India, 19th c. Collection Ajit Mookerjee.

Interplay

The *t'ai chi*, or the supreme interplay of Yang and Yin, of male and female, of mountain and valley, produces, according to the *I Ching*, the surrounding trigrams of archetypal differentiation and manifestation. The secret of its creativity lies in the female dot at the centre of its male part, and in the male centre of its female part. The circle rotates because the core of each half is of the same nature as the rest of the other half, and seeks to reunite with it. The rotation is clockwise, towards the valley, the mother. Therefore the pliant and humble is destined to prevail. By 'becoming the valley', says the *Tao tē ching* (I, 28), one musters strength and becomes resilient like a child. By remaining in the darkness of the valley, one measures all things from a distance, and 'becomes the yardstick'; one's strength becomes stable and one identifies with the absolute.

The two halves of the *t'ai chi* are shaped like twin embryos, the head of one touching the feet of the other. Their salient or throbbing points urge them back to the undivided, original state; yet this movement towards amalgamation

results in further differentiation: the life- and death-instincts are inseparable.

This interplay of the elements of the universe can be represented in a picture, and by meditating on it one achieves identification with the cosmic laws. Metaphysics is expounded through such designs even more effectively than with words. Vedanta may be inwardly assimilated by becoming absorbed in *Jambu dvip* (below left), the map of the universe as the field of the primal essen-

tial energies, which through androgyne amalgamations produce constant changes on the various levels of being. Zodiacal cosmic man is an illustration of the global interplay between sexual differentiation and androgyny. The four operations of alchemy, the four humours and the four seasons are apportioned to the four quarters of the figure. From phlegm (female upper quarter) the essential oils, corresponding to blood and to the soul, are distilled (male upper

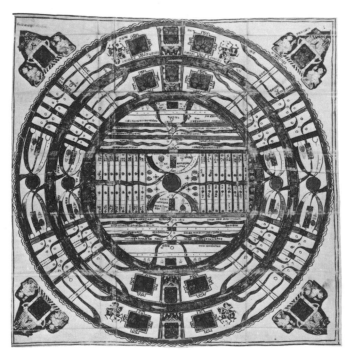

quarter); from the remaining phlegm fermentation releases the spirit (lower male quarter) and finally the solid residue, the body (lower female quarter) can be calcinated to ashes (see pp. 80–81).

Giordano Bruno in the sixteenth century produced the best Western counterparts of Vedantic mandalas (see *De monade numero et figura*, in Bruno 1884, pp. 349, 380–6, 402ff.). The simplest representation of androgyny that he offers consists of two interlocking circles, whose common section was known in Western traditional art as the fish's eye or the almond. Artists placed within it Christ and the Virgin in glory, because it is the space in which two are one.

Androgyny is best symbolized, Bruno taught, by the pentad ✩ which corresponds to a man with arms extended and legs spread out. The head represents God, the movement from an origin, the mind; the right arm the intellect as the self-reflection of the mind; the eye, the movement towards a medium. The left arm is the soul, the means, focussing. The right leg the principle of form, the movement from the means to the end, time and recoil. The left leg matter, the end, attraction and space. The five fingers of the hand and the five main lines of the palm (Heart, Life, Head, Destiny and Mars) can also be traced on the pentad. The number five represents androgyny, being the sum of (female) two and (male) three (see also p. 5).

Left-hand page:
The t'ai chi. Octagonal ink-cake by Ch'eng Chung-fan, China, 17th c. Private collection.

Jambu dvip. Gouache on cloth, India, 15th c. Courtesy Jean Claude Ciancimino, London.

Zodiacal cosmic man. From Leonhart Thurneisser zum Thurn, *Quinta essentia*, Leipzig, 1574.

Right-hand page:
Interlocking circles. From Giordano Bruno, *De monade numero et figura*, Frankfurt, 1591. British Library, London.

Pentagonal figure. From Giordano Bruno, *De monade numero et figura*, Frankfurt, 1591. British Library, London.

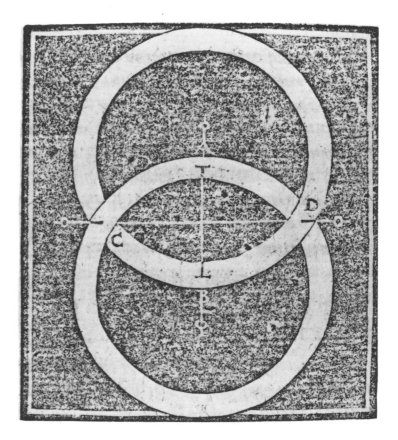

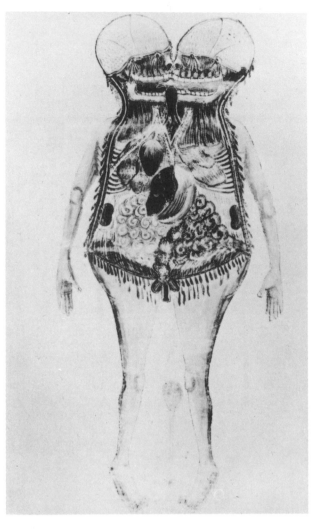

The split

Man's life can be defined as the constant and endless process of healing an inner split. Astoundingly, the idea is implied in the medieval drawing of the human body and brain, suggesting some degree of knowledge of the brain's division into two hemispheres and of their interplay in the bodily system. On a theological level this would have also conveyed, to a medieval mind, the sexual nature of the split, because the soul and the brain were supposed to be divided into a feminine, sensory part on one hand and masculine reason and will on the other.

The Śivaite idea of life is that of a constant process of splitting and healing. When the goddess stalks out of androgyne Śiva she leaves him with an aching side, but Śiva reabsorbs her constantly. Androgyne Śiva is silvered with ash, pupil upturned in ecstasy on his right, male side, and yellowed with saffron, gazing at the onlooker on his left female side. He is the essence of creativity, being the semen-thrower and the womb at the same time. Semen itself is identified with Brahma. The story is told that Brahma the Creator engendered a female to couple with, but thereby lost his power to create, *sṛṣṭiśakti*. (The moral may be Blakean: by forgetting that it is we ourselves who imagine and project outer reality onto existence, we lose our projective power.) It was then that

death entered the world. Brahma resorted to yoga and developed such inner heat (*tapas*), that he evoked Śiva, who appeared in his female form. Creativity was restored to Brahma, but in the process he too became female.

A perpetual process of life-giving androgynization goes on in the atmosphere, as is shown in the Indian drawing of fire and water coupling in mid-air, According to alchemy, earthly moisture, suspended in the air and impregnated by the moon, blends with the solar rays, and two subtle androgyne essences are born, Mercurius, the essence of transmutations, and salt, the fixating agent, which together, after giving life to plants in the form of dew, penetrate the earth, in which they become the seed of metals. It should be noticed that fire and water in the drawing have eight arms. The fusion can take place only if it is effected through a double decussation, or crossing. In a stable society, cross-cousin marriages tend to be institutionalized, and correspond to the transition from a superficial to a four-square affirmation of androgyny. This might also explain why the freak of the hermaphrodite Siamese twins with their double sex organs in reverse order should appear not wholly unpleasant to the eye.

The Renaissance image of androgynization (above right) also teaches the lesson of fusion through decussation. The lusting of the two opposites for one another (emblemized by the dog) produces a spiral (symbolized by the coils of the serpent, by the chain being tugged in opposite directions by the two cupids, and by the motif of entwining vines in the background). This is possible because the solar thrust, represented by the male's winged feet, keeps him contracted in his effort (symbolized by the female holding over his head a bird with folded wings), while the female becomes volatile (the male holding over *her* a bird with outspread wings). The androgyne fusion spirals upward only in the presence of criss-crossing currents, similar to the actual chiasma of the eye-nerves. (C. G. Jung stressed that in an intimate encounter between a man and a woman there is always a decussation between the man and his feminine soul, or anima, on the one side and the woman and her male soul, or animus, on the other.)

Longing for unity

The *Bṛhadaranyaka Upaniṣad* (IV. 3. 21) states that 'as in the arms of a beloved woman one knows nothing more of the outward or of the inner, in the human person (*puruṣa*) embraced by the all-knowing absolute (*prajñātmanā*), all longings (*kama*) are fulfilled, only the longing for the absolute subsists, all desire and sorrow disappear.'

The emblem of marriage from Barthélemy Aneau's *Picta poesis* shows how far these notions were alive in the Western Renaissance. Man and wife are united by a true-love's-knot and become one with the tree of life, which is also signified by the cross they form with their arms. (Moses and a Satyr in the background may represent control and impulse, Law and Nature.) It has been pointed out (by D. Cheney) that the scene is similar to Spenser's encounter (*The Faerie Queene*, Bk 3, 1590 edn) between Amoret and her husband, who are said to recall Salmakis and Hermaphroditus (see pp. 29, 45). Britomart looks on 'half envying their blisses', and 'much empassioned in their gentle sprites': half approving Moses, half ogling Satyr, or, in Spenserian terms, part devotee of Diana, part woman tempted by Venus.

The celebration of androgynous love as the golden mean between jealousy, or excess, and rejection or lack of love forms the subject of the Greek fountain at the gate of Gallipoli. Three myths are represented, with a commentary of three Latin epigraphs. The first tells the story of Dirce, the devotee of Dionysus who out of jealousy confined Antiope to a dungeon. Antiope's twin sons, Amphion the songster and Zethus the herdsman, grew up and avenged their mother by tying Dirce by her hair to a savage bull. At the spot where her mangled body lay, Dionysus caused a spring to gush out of the earth. He is shown standing above her, with the comment: 'Jealous fury avoid, you who drink of this frenzy.'

At the opposite end of the fountain is carved the myth of Byblis. She fell in love with her brother, and when he fled in horror she pursued him until she broke down on the way, and her tears formed a pool. She is shown lying on the ground, her brother above her, in flight ('O suck this sweet pap, unhappy love spouts old hatreds').

Between the two extremes of jealousy and revulsion, stands the relief of Venus bringing together Salmakis and Hermaphroditus (see p. 44), with Cupid in attendance. The epigraph is a quotation from Ausonius: 'Happy virgin she, if she know that man is within her. / But twice-happy you, my lad, merging with the lovely girl, / If two can be one thing'.

Above runs a bas-relief of Hercules at grips with the Nemean lion and the Lernean hydra, his first and second labours. Between Leo and Cancer, assault and retreat, wrath and disdain, stands androgyny.

The perfect blending was symbolized by the love of Hermes and Aphrodite, from which Hermaphroditus was born. Michael Maier comments on the engraving, stressing that Hermaphroditus corresponds to Parnassus, the two-peaked mountain, where Apollo dwells with the Muses, and through which passes the axis of the world. This seems to correspond to the spine of Cosmic Man and to the serpent Kundalini uncoiling through it. These correlations between sexual fusion and the essence of the cosmos which in the West were only cryptically hinted at in alchemical treatises such as Maier's, in Hindu temples were taught quite openly.

In Śivaite Tantra, the preferred form of ritual intercourse is *viparītarata*, with the female above the male. The same preference is shown in the iconology of the loves of Rādha and Kṛṣṇa. When Hermes and Aphrodite come together, the male should likewise be beneath the female, for both alchemical and astrological reasons (Taurus comes before Gemini). 'The wingless male is under the winged female. Therefore it is said: Cast the female upon the male, subsequently the male shall climb over the female' (Senior, *De chemia*, Strasbourg 1566). The traditional icon will be spontaneously reproduced by a pair of dancers, if they happen to enter into the spirit of androgyny.

Left-hand page:
Fountain at Gallipoli. Stone, Italy.

Emblem on marriage. Woodcut from Barthélemy Aneau, *Picta poesis*, Lyon, 1552. British Library, London.

Right-hand page:
Hermes and Aphrodite. From Michael Maier, *Atalanta fugiens*, Frankfurt, 1617.

Jacques Garnier and Brigitte LeFèvre performing *Pas de Deux*, choreographed by Jacques Garnier, Le Théâtre du Silence, La Rochelle, France.

Couple in sexual intercourse. Stone sculpture from the heaven bands of the Devi Jagdambu temple at Khajurāho, India.

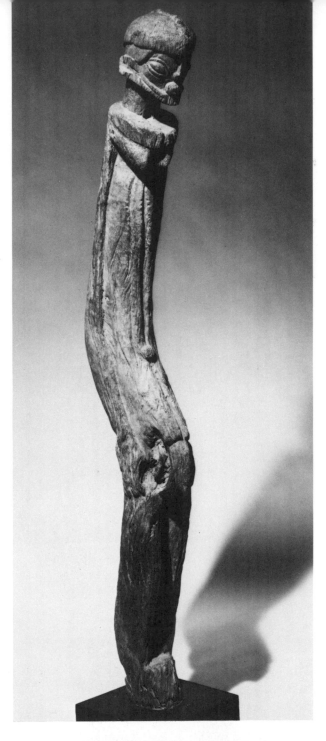

The hermaphrodite

In African religions, as in ancient Egypt, androgyny is a common trait of creator gods. The first Ancestors are androgyne since they alone give birth to their stock; tricksters and divinities of the crossroads participate in either sex. The African traditional outlook is based on the balancing of pairs which carry sexual overtones: the lower/higher and the right/left sides in objects, the alternatives of hot and cold, seed and fruit.

In India Śiva is essentially androgyne even when his aspect is male. In the hymn devoted to him at the opening of the Tamil Sangha Anthology, it is said that 'Half his body enfolds the opposite sex, / His form sucks it in and hides it up'.

When his dual nature is displayed, he is called Ardhanārīśvara, male-female Lord (see also p. 19) and to Tantric practitioners symbolizes the state of *samarasa*, the 'flavour of sameness', in which breathing and thinking cease and semen is stayed (he is here represented as ithyphallic). Ardhanārīśvara is often shown swaying, and pushing out his-her left hip. When the vertical sexual division in the androgyne is stressed with contrary movements of the arms and legs, an ecstatic whirl is suggested (below right). In the Greco-Roman world a distinction can be made between androgyne figures that are vertically divided and Hermaphroditus, born of Hermes and Aphrodite, who was divided horizontally – male below the waist and female above it. In the round of the zodiac, Hermes-Mercury, in both Gemini and Virgo, is preceded by Aphrodite-Venus in Taurus and in Libra respectively. Hermaphroditus was given his two particular seasons, being a god of flowers and fruits, of sex and vegetation.

Left-hand page:
Hermaphrodite statue of the Dogon.
Wood, Mali. Musée de l'Homme, Paris.

Hermaphrodite figure. Ivory, Zaire.

Androgynous child reported from
Africa. Woodcut from Conrad
Lycosthenes, *Prodigiorum ac ostentorum
chronicon*, Basel, 1557.

Right-hand page:
Hermaphrodite statue. Greece.
Nationalmuseum, Stockholm.

Ardhanārīśvara. Stone, India, 12th c.
Indian Museum, Calcutta.

Hermes

Encountering snakes mating is the most favourable omen among many peoples. In the myth of Teiresias (see pp. 18–20), it starts him on his course of androgynization and seership. In Yoga and Tantra the motif of the enlacing serpents represents the perfect balancing of inner energies. Tingling backbones, poised snakes, erect phalluses all belong together. When shrill notes ripple forth, spines shiver in reply; a tune working itself up in spirals, played on a flute or rolled on a drum or danced to by sleek, lithe limbs, raises phalluses and snakes alike. The peculiar, complete ecstasy of androgyny is typified by the caduceus which, as a representation of snakes mating, denotes the correspondence, section by section, of the androgyne being with the cosmos. The path of the zodiac can be projected onto a caduceus:

In the Western tradition Giordano Bruno spoke in *De immenso et innumerabili* (VI, 5) of coupling serpents interpenetrating each other as an emblem of Sun-Dionysus being embraced by Earth-Ceres. The solar rays, he says, enter the womb of earthly moisture to reach down, eternally, to the very femur of the cosmic mother. Flutes are made from femurs.

To relate to this core of cosmic life is the aim of the adept, both as an alchemist and as a mystic. He identifies himself with Mercurius, the fluid androgyne principle of reality. First of all, Mercurius slumbers, abstracting himself from waking reality (left), in order to dream the right dreams. His subtle body then rises as a caduceus from his groin (also denoting REM sleep, leading to erection). The principle of light and warmth hovers above him. In the following phase he is crowned, the caduceus now rises perpendicularly and touches the heart centre, where sun and moon mate androgynously. One foot rests on fire and the other on earth. In the third

picture the transformation is achieved; Mercurius is now the perfected androgyne, holding the orb of Empire in his left hand and the caduceus in the right. The caduceus is now externalized, bringing harmony no longer only to the inner man, but projecting it outwards, imparting it to the world. Saturn and the Moon, Jupiter and Mercury, Mars and Venus finally blend one with the other and all together, and Mercurius carries them as a bouquet of flowers into the bowels of the earth, where they will become the souls of lead and silver, tin and mercury, iron and copper respectively, a spiral culminating in solar gold.

Duccio's Mercury (this page) is shown at the peak of his power, the stars in the background signifying the harmony of the spheres. (The details must have been suggested by the hermetists who had gathered at the court of Sigismondo Malatesta.) Souls are led in and out of the earth by the magic wand, the cock of vigilance is perched on the left foot, the conical cap of wizardry rises heavenward above the androgyne brow, while the clouds floating round the knees convey, as Adrian Stokes remarked (in *The Stones of Rimini*, Stokes 1978), the swirl of an upward-rising vortex. The right, masculine foot rests on the rock, from which fire can be struck; the feminine, left foot is dipped in female waters.

Left-hand page:
The caduceus raised from the groin. From Urbigerus, Germany, 17th c. (in *Quinta essentia*, VI, Oberarth, 1977).

The caduceus terminating at the heart. Codex, Italy, 17th c. From *Conoscenza religiosa*, 1, Florence, 1980. Biblioteca Medicea Laurenziana, Florence.

The final phase of androgynization. From Urbigerus, in *Quinta essentia*, VII.

Mercurius descending into the bowels of the earth. From Urbigerus, in *Quinta essentia*, III.

Right-hand page:
Mercury. Relief sculpture by Agostino di Duccio at Tempio Malatestiano, Rimini. Italy, 15th c.

The alchemical androgyne

Hermes Trismegistus, the legendary founder of alchemy, points to the primal mystery in nature, the principle of fire, which enfolds in its fourfold flames the two essential opposites, sun and moon, male and female, sulphur and mercury (right), which become the one androgyne at all moments of conception and birth in nature. They surround the earth (below), gathering into it the astral influences, and at its core combine in the form of a triangle (or rather, three-dimensionally, of a pyramid, which is the shape of a crystal of salt – both the male salts of the sea and the female alums of clay). The right side of the triangle symbolizes the male sulphurous principle, its left side the female mercurial principle, and its base the principle of salt. The square and the circle hint at the squaring of the circle, which is a symbol for androgyny. The progression is therefore from the triangle to the square to the circle. Nature is one in all its three realms – the aerial, vegetable and animal, and mineral, worlds because in each one of them it is the same mating of the opposites that produces harmony, the same solar and lunar principles coming together. The mating can be visualized (opposite left) as a serpent (nature) with a lion's head (devouring fire and putrefaction) and a tail in the shape of an eagle's head (volatility) in the act of extracting from itself the invisible and impalpable moisture, by which the finest elements of the

body are compacted together: in it lies the power of the sun and of the moon, which the serpent is shown squeezing through its coils (see also p. pp. 80–81).

The process is threefold. It starts with a first, embryonic androgyne phase, which in the case of mineral bodies takes place when in the bowels of the earth a nitrous, salty soil ⊖ is impregnated with an acrid, corrosive vapour (♁ and ☿); the two are gathered together by the principles of sunlight which enter the earth in the form of dew. The same dew that nourishes the life of plants can also activate this volatility beneath the earth. The result is called primal matter, or Rebis, or fiery androgyne (both principles being acrid and burning), or Adam (because they are the first engendering principle in the

mineral world). Isaac Newton preferred 'Chaos'. Paracelsus joked, calling it 'Tree-and-Apple' (opposite above) or Girl Pip ⊖ and Boy Pulp ♁ (the king and queen near the tree). The pulp will rot off, burn out in time, only to be remade out of the substance of the girl (the moons). The root of the process is often called the Poisonous Dragon. In the androgyne opposite below it is a cloud of goats' heads, with boy and girl uncoiling out of the goats' beards to curl up the two legs of the androgyne. We find the same symbolism of the goat in India, where the word *ajā* ('goat' in Sanscrit), can also mean 'unborn', and therefore nature (which below the earth is both fetid and ebullient).

Why not give this substance one name, and stick to it? This is not possible

because it is not necessarily cinnabar or sulphuretted antimony or anything else as such. To look for the chemical equivalent of the androgyne of fire is to go on a wild goose chase. The androgyne is a global situation, it 'happens' when the principle of light, of sun and moon, is caught in the grip of a crude, poisonous soil and starts fermenting.

In a second phase, saltpetre vapours get to work, corroding and subtilizing the androgyne, which now puffs up the earth and whisks off the vapours that have penetrated it, purifying them in the process and making them fluid. This is called the bath of the androgyne, or royal couple. It is followed by the third and final phase, when out of the mess a glassy, viscous paste emerges, called the 'Philosophers' Stone' or 'Pearl' or 'Fish's Eye' or 'First Magnet' (because it attracts all it needs from the surrounding soil).

Left-hand page:
Hermes Trismegistus. From Michael Maier, *Symbola aureae mensae*, Frankfurt, 1617.

The two essential opposites combining as a triangle. From J. D. Mylius, *Philosophia reformata*, Frankfurt, 1617.

The uniting of opposites. From Michael Maier, *Atalanta fugiens*, Frankfurt, 1617.

Right-hand page:
Nature as serpent. From Daniel Stolcius, *Viridarium chymicum*, Frankfurt, 1624.

The rebirth of primal matter. From J. D. Mylius, *Philosophia reformata*, Frankfurt, 1622.

Androgyne with goats' heads. Codex germanicus Monacensis, Cgm 598, f.106v, Germany, 15th c. Bayerisches Staatsbibliothek, Munich.

6. *Solutio.*

The alchemical androgyne (cont'd)

Alchemists call the substance that compacts the male and the female principles in nature together resin, and they consider it to be the energizing of the sulphurous principle, ♀. In his treatise *Antibarbarus* (Berlin, 1894), August Strindberg describes how resin can be revealed in the form of turpentine, of guttapercha, of common sulphur fried in a pan, or in nascent gold. Resin is simply the proof of a perfect amalgamation of the androgyne, resulting in the pure, fluid essence of gold (not common gold, which is the mere trace in dead matter of a perfect androgyne resinous amalgamation). The picture from Urbigerus (above left) shows the androgyne substance on the left in its first, and on the right in its second phase (see p. 79), after it has taken its 'bath' in what appears to be the resin percolating from a hole in the counterpart of the tree of life in the world of metals. This hole can also be represented as a green lion biting the sun (above right), especially when the work is done on regulus of antimony (see p. 35). The vapours of the androgyne are collected in a fluid state from an oven in which the conditions of the second phase are reproduced (see p. 79). The process is represented by a flaming man (the ore) and by a woman who is pointing to the symbolic lion and sun, comparing the ascent of the pith in a tree to the extraction of the fluids. The third phase can be shown as the new substance resting upon its mother's lap (right), as an em-

bryo filling up the belly of the androgyne which is being subjected to the ablutions of the second phase (opposite above right), or as an androgyne son (opposite above left).

A global picture of the alchemical view of nature is shown opposite below as two main processes: to the left the calcination of bodies and to the right

the distillation of essences (of souls and spirits). This is true of all realms of nature, but it is easier to illustrate in the case of a plant. The ethereal oils are its solar soul (sulphur ♀), the alcohol is its lunar spirit (Mercurius ☿). These are seen as male and female, accompanied by their lions, entering Hermes' cave. The plant is crushed, its oils separated

COLOR CŒLESTINUS.

COLOR CŒLESTINUS.
cum tua terra nigra.

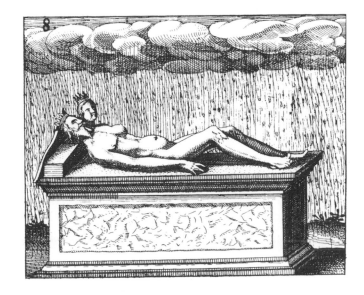

and its spirit distilled in a retort (the pelican); their rising vapours are represented as an eagle soaring heavenward, holding them in its claws – the world of the soul and that of the spirit. In high heaven, at the final phase of the operation, they are mixed together, and form the Turtle Dove of perfect love.

On the other side of the Tree of Life, the dark residue of the plant, which remains at the bottom of the still (the raven), is cooked (by the fire of Mars ♂) until it loses its lead-like character (the sign of Saturn ♄) and acquires a tin-like hue (the sign of Jupiter ♃), the silvery colour of ash (the white swan). The ashes are treated with 'resins' and fire, until their salt loosens its 'radical moisture' (as happens with ashes in the fabrication of glass). This is emblemized by the eye-bespangled peacock (which in wintertime looks like a mere crow) and even more appropriately by the Phoenix (which feeds on resins and burns itself up in order to be reborn). The Phoenix rises from its ashes, clutching two worlds in its claws, the earth and the fire of the process, and in the final phase in high heaven, it becomes the pure lamb of sacrifice. Here the calcinated body (the dead Phoenix) is imbued with the fluid tincture (the dead Turtle Dove), until they coalesce into the Stone of the Plant (Philosophers' Stone), the plant in its purest and most essential form. Shakespeare wrote a poem about all this, *The Phoenix and the Turtle*, in honour of the two birds that have died and become one.

Left-hand page:
The androgyne substance in its first and second phases. From *Quinta essentia*, II, Oberarth, 1976.

Collecting the vapours of the androgyne. From Michael Maier, *Symbola aureae mensae*, Frankfurt, 1617.

The androgyne substance in its third phase. From J. D. Mylius, *Anatomiae auri*, Frankfurt, 1628.

Right-hand page:
The androgyne son. From J. D. Mylius, *Anatomiae auri*, Frankfurt, 1628.

The substance in the belly of an androgyne. From J. D. Mylius, *Philosophia reformata*, Frankfurt, 1622.

The two alchemical processes of nature. From *Microcosmos hypochondriacus* (*Microcosmi physicomathematici*), Perugia, 1658. British Library, London.

The bisexual shaman

The transvestism of the priest is a normal feature of many cults, but the training of the shaman may even result in a bodily trans-sexual condition. There are many reasons for shamanic sex-reversal. Among Siouan tribes it is motivated by a desire to identify with the moon; this is also the reason for Orphic transvestism. Among the Araucanian shamans studied by Métraux, the aim of sex reversal is to identify with the bi-sexual Supreme Creator. In other cases it is the acquisition of special magical powers, especially ventriloquy.

The order to change dress and habits comes from a spirit, which wishes to teach the shaman the art of attracting people of her/his own sex. It may also be a spirit seeking a wife or a husband, or a spirit of the opposite sex to the shaman which requires a complete identification with itself.

Institutionalized religious sex reversal among American Indians was noticed by early travellers, who called the practitioners *berdaches*, probably from the Italian *baldracca*, 'whore'. No detailed account has been preserved of their peculiar shamanic practices, and among the very few documents of the custom are photographs of some of the last trans-sexual practitioners (left, below and opposite below). The tradition dates back to the very first settlers, at least in the Colorado region – witness the cave drawing of a dancer identifying with a mythical horned and double-sexed creature. The tradition is carried on even today among esoteric native societies, as in the case of María Sabina, one of the very few fairly well documented cases of shamanic androgynization (see also pp. 12–14).

S. Frazão, a Portuguese student of Angolan cults, has provided us with a rare account of androgynization dances: those of the Mila Mila society (see Frazão 1946). The sessions are supposed to cure obsessions and depressions caused by spirits. They start with the sacrifice of an animal, and everybody drinks of its still-warm blood. The dance that follows resembles the jig or the tarantella. At its peak the spirits take possession of the dancers, after the priest has touched their tongue with the tooth of a cobra. It may take months for the possession to wear off. While it lasts, women behave like men, taking one or more wives, and men dress like women and live with youths. A refusal to become their brides or bridegrooms would mean disrespect towards the spirits. Nobody remembers what occurred during possession, and homosexuality is normally absent from the tribe. The peculiar stock of knowledge acquired through the period of initiatory possession is, on the other hand, remembered clearly and prized by the adepts as their supreme treasure.

Losing one's head

The new Aries sun shining after the
thaws and floods of Pisces was pictured
as a young solar hero beheading a
female water monster whose gaze had
frozen nature stiff during the winter
months. Perseus, the solar hero, held up
the slimy head of Medusa, with its
bulging eyes and snake-like curls.
Sometimes Medusa is actually shown as
a floating hydra-like head or as a
bearded woman or as a triad of fish, a
variation on the usual Piscean pair.

For the situation on the opposite side
of the zodiac the picture is reversed: at
the autumn equinox a young lunar
goddess of crops beheads the vege-
tation hero: Virgo, the Corn Maiden is
shown holding forth his severed head
(or simply an ear of wheat), just as the
priestess did at the rituals of Eleusis. In
Christian times the ear of wheat becomes the head of St John the Baptist
raised high on a platter by autumnal
Salomé-Herodias (see also pp. 22–23).
The autumn maiden might well be the
very same old springtime crone, just as
the prophet slain at the oncoming of
autumn might well be the now aged
hero and baptizer. Traces of these cross-
equinoxial identifications remain in
Greek myth: Medusa is one of the
names for Proserpine, the Corn
Maiden; she is said to wear a Medusa
mask when she inhabits the nether-
world; Perseus cuts off Medusa's head
with a golden sickle; she used the sickle
on him in the autumn, and he is now
retaliating.

But there are more ways than one to
slay a dragon, and the story may run
that springtime prince charming made
love to the loathly hag, who lost her
head over the treat, and vice versa with
the aging hero when the maiden fell for
him in the autumn. These loves are of an
unusual or ill-fated kind: the hag of
Pisces, suffering Venus, can be bearded;
there is a hint of womanliness in certain
St Johns. Modern literature has been

attracted time and again to the
sexlessness of the lunar prophet. Long
before Oscar Wilde laboured lushly at
the idea of Salomé-Herodias' passion for
the unresponsive Baptist, Heine had
detected the love behind her hatred of
him. Mallarmé imagined her as a jewel-
eyed virgin of a starry, metallic,
quivering chastity: an unhappy seeker of
androgyny, a reptile huddled up in 'an
inner night of icicles and snow' (see p. 7).

Left-hand page:
Medusa head. From *Folk-Lore*, XIV, 3, published by the Folk-lore Society, London, 1903.

Head of a Martyr. Charcoal drawing by Odilon Redon, France, 19th c. Kröller-Müller Foundation, Otterlo.

St John the Baptist. Chalk drawing by Leonardo da Vinci, Italy, 16th c.

Right-hand page:
The hag of Pisces. From *Folk-Lore*, XIV, 3, published by the Folk-lore Society, London, 1903.

Triad of fish. Ornament from a menology, Armenia, 15th c. Bibliothèque Nationale, Paris.

Enlightenment Beyond the Crown of the Head. Gouache on paper, India, 18th c. Collection Ajit Mookerjee.

Chinnamastā Durgā. Gouache on paper, India, 18th–19th c. Collection Ajit Mookerjee.

The song Mallarmé placed on the lips of St John the Baptist tells, on the contrary, of a successful quest; his gaze is said to emerge beyond the bonds of his body, and even to rise beyond the intoxication of fasts, and beyond icy apathy, so that he is finally 'enlightened at the same/Principle which chose *him*'. The peak experience which the song endeavours to describe is represented by the Rajasthani painting of 'enlightenment beyond the crown of the head', in which the adept loses his head, beyond the duality of sun and moon.

In India the whole coupled quaternion Medusa-with-Perseus and St John-with-Herodias is summed up in Durgā the Beheaded (Chinnamastā Durgā), who cuts off her crowned head while standing upon her own crownless body, which lies coupling with crowned Śiva. In her left hand she holds her severed head, letting the blood (the source of all desires), drip into a cup, usually a skull, held by Kali ('Destruction'), while in her right hand she flourishes the knife of discrimination; the blood that drips from it is collected by Mahakali ('Total extinction'), symbolizing the merging of ascetic activity (*rajas*) into the sheer awareness of being (*sattva*). Temple priestesses were married to Durgā's blade (see also p. 23), which corresponds to the 'sword of chastity' placed between lovers in Celtic lore.

The plunge

Taking off from a cliff into roaring, froth-
ing waters is to dare the powers of
death. In a magical world-view, the diver
who comes up unscathed proves his
good luck. In fact his deed is supposed
to enhance it and gain him favour with
the gods. Such a leap into treacherous
waves bespeaks assurance and sur-
render, a readiness for self-sacrifice. In
Hindu scriptures, the sea is where 'name
and likeness are dissolved' (see also p.
23). When everything turns out well, the
god is taken to have accepted the
offering. One is redeemed.

The ritual plunge was put to practical
uses when it became a form of judicial
ordeal, a deferral of judgment to the
water god or a handy way of disposing
of scapegoats. It is found all over the
world, from China to the ancient Middle
East. Judiciaries, however, differ as to
how the god's language is to be read; in
India innocents had better do their best
to keep afloat, while suspects of witch-
craft in Europe do well to sink.

In its heyday the rite must have
wrought wonderful transformations in
the diver. In Lesbos and Etruria, for
example, a special clergy trained the
candidate's body and imagination, and

provided instruction in the myths before administering the sacrament. One suspects that an intoxicating herb was given to eat or drink; Pliny hints at it when speaking of Sappho, the most famous of divers. The flight from off the cliff must have been accompanied by an experience not unusual in the imminence of death, that of reliving one's whole life in a flash. The soul was scoured. A force hitherto unknown was felt to rise from nowhere, out of the depths of one's being. It took over in the nick of time, in the teeth of death. One now identified with this saving force and became a new man, and, the texts hint, an androgyne.

This androgyny was signified by sacrificing a boy and a girl, throwing them together into the sea at Tenedos and at Chryse in Troas. This custom originated from the myth of Tenes, who was thrown to the waves with his sister. I surmise he was no other than the Egyptian god Ten, the androgyne Creator whose sister Neit bore his name in reverse, and had a phallus.

The diver in mid-air on the Paestum tomb seems to be enacting the ritual jump, as seen also in the murals of Etruscan tombs.

In the apse of the Pythagorean Basilica in Rome a stucco relief shows Sappho having taken her leap off the white cliff of Lesbos, assisted by Apollo the Sun and lyre-player, the same Apollo who is depicted as a hermaphrodite in an ancient painting at the Museo Barracco in Rome. The legend runs that the poetess was seeking to transcend an earthly love – the plunge is said to assuage the sorrows of love.

The archetype can catch in its grip any free-wheeling intoxicated mind. It happened with two drunken lovers on a windy English September day in 1980; *The Times* of 6 September reported that they slipped as if in a kind of trance, and yet deliberately, through a fence to the brink of a cliff; there they cuddled and hugged each other, rolling over and over, until suddenly the man turned over and span off the edge to his death – bringing the ritual back to life. The archetype is always there, lurking within us.

The theatrical jump can even be dispensed with. The bath is enough, provided the waters whisk into a liquid maze. Emblematic eddies and undercurrents, pulls in opposite directions, are requisites. The toss above must be answered with a tug from the undertow, so as to tilt and spin the bather off to the proper symbolic conclusion – personified in Greek myth by the union of the water nymph Salmakis and Hermaphroditus (see also pp. 44–45). In India, a song attributed to Candidas speaks of the currents of the lake of love: 'when they are joined in one, the truth of union is realized'.

Left-hand page:
Sappho flinging herself from a cliff. Stucco decoration on the apse of the Basilica Sotteranea, Porta Maggiore, Rome. Italy.

Sappho Flinging Herself into the Sea. Watercolour by Gustave Moreau, France, 19th c. Private collection, Paris.

The tomb of the diver. Paestum. Fresco, Italy, 5th c. BC.

Right-hand page:
The Nymph Salmakis Descends into the Pool to Surprise Hermaphroditus. Oil painting by Francesco Albani. Italy, 17th c. Galleria Sabauda, Torino.

Alchemical sun and moon. From Michael Maier, *Atalanta fugiens,* Frankfurt, 1617.

Head to foot

Oedipus answers the sphinx (above left), whose riddle can be found in an extended form and with a purely metaphysical turn in a passage of a hymn of the *Atharva Veda* (X. 8, 27–8) addressed to the One Being or World Embryo, the Primal Engenderer or Cosmic Man, Prajāpati who is an adult male or female, a boy or a girl, an old man leaning on a stick or a new-born baby gazing all around him-her, father of all and son of all. Other texts describe Prajāpati as sightless and footless (*apad*), sacrificer and sacrificed. These characters correspond to events in Oedipus's life (see pp. 19–20), so he not only gives but *is* the answer to the riddle of the sphinx. His destiny is a pantomime describing symbolically the essential features of

Cosmic Man. Greek mythographers reduced a weird-looking archaic metaphysical icon to tragic pseudo-history, in which the various original motifs only partially survive. The story, as it is preserved, insists rather strangely on a pin that was driven through baby Oedipus's feet and on a thorn which he stuck at the turning point of his life through his eyes. An icon of blighted feet and head suggests itself – the needle of fate threading them together, to typify the primordial embryo or androgyne, head to foot and self-sufficient to the point of not needing external sight (like Dīrghatamas of the *Ṛg Veda*, 'Longdarkness').

The end of the year fell under Pisces, which ruled the feet, while its beginning lay under the Ram, which ruled the head (opposite above); man becomes the icon of the year (which is Prajāpati) by touching his feet to his head (below

left). The head of St John the Baptist, the inaugurator of the new dispensation (see p. 57) rolls at the feet of his sacrificers (opposite below). The head of the arch-androgyne Teiresias (see pp. 18–20), the pivotal figure who sparks Oedipus's destiny, the all-knowing blind seer, the Greek 'Longdarkness', is evoked from the nether-world, from the realm of the past, of Pisces, to speak the truth at the feet of the sacrificer, head to head with the sacrificial Ram (above right).

In the ancient world dancers at mournings bent over backward, heads to feet. They went back to the state of potential being, to how they had been when curled up in a slushy womb, feet touching the throbbing brain-pan. It was felt to be significant that in battle the wounded should twist backward into death, and that the same position should be struck in spirit possession.

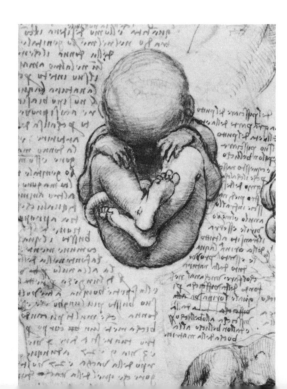

Twisting into a ball – reminiscent of
shrove-tide footballs, of the silver balls
of shrove-tide hurlings at the junction of
Pisces and Aries – is a ritual evocation of
the mythical circular androgyne that
Plato mentions in his *Symposium*, and of
the spherical cosmic man of his
Timaeus, who, being all-comprising,
needs neither eyes nor feet. He has
nothing to gain or learn from the outside world. Among the Church fathers,
Origen believed that resurrected bodies
would be circular, going back to the
Adamic state. At the peak of Paradise,
Dante described omniscient Adam in all
his splendour and cries: 'O apple, you
who alone were created ripe'. Adam is
'the first engenderer' (a literal translation
of 'Prajāpati'), 'the man who was not
born', he adds in *Convivio* (IV,XV, 3).
Adam was male and female in one,
before God plunged him into a fatal
swoon (see p. 40). Alchemists interpreted this in terms of mineralogy: in
the seventeenth century Henricus
Khunrath explained that the form of
saltiness is round, being light coagu-
lated, . It is the bond and the
destroyer of everything, the 'Catholic
[Universal] Androgyne'.

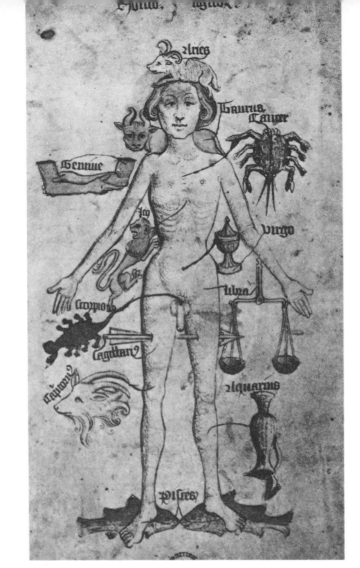

Left-hand page:
Oedipus solves the riddle of the Sphinx.
Painted medallion from an Attic dish,
Greece, 5th c. BC. Museo Etrusco
Gregoriano, Rome.

Ulysses encounters Teiresias. Drawing of
a scene on a vase, Greece, 5th c. BC.
Bibliothèque Nationale, Paris.

Hindu Zodiacal man. India. From
Chakra, A Journal of Tantra and Yoga,
New Delhi, 1972.

Human foetus. Drawing by Leonardo da
Vinci, Italy, 16th c.

Right-hand page:
Zodiacal man. Ms illustration from *The
Guildbook of Barber Surgeons of York,*
England, 16th c. British Library, London.

The execution of St John the Baptist.
Detail of Panel XVI of the South Door of
the Florence Baptistery Doors, Italy, 14th c.
Photograph by David Finn, from K.
Clark, D. Finn and G. Robinson, *The
Florence Baptistery Doors*, London, 1980.

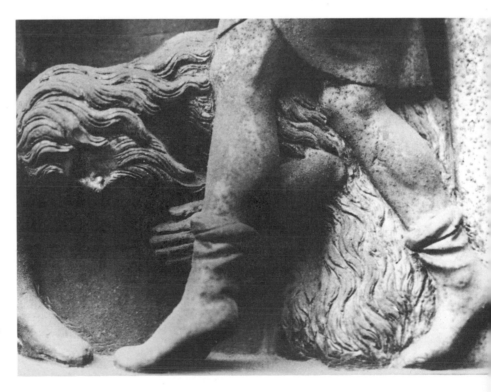

Carnival, when men get pregnant

Under the sign of Pisces, spent out Sun has run his course, having sired on Mother Earth/Moon twelve months in succession. At this time his unhealthy, thirteenish rays lack warmth and light. Men pass this month as if it were one long wake of mingled iambic dirges and preposterous merry-making. The body of the old Sun is felt to be stretched out and having to be attended to. At wakes, such as may still be witnessed in the Rumanian countryside, lamentations are for the daytime – shadows forbid mourning, and lack of sleep is good for depression, so there remains little to do at night but to tell stories and then start playing scandalous carnival games. In England the London synod of 1342 put an end to love-making at wakes.

The sign of Pisces, the wake of the year, is, however, still celebrated. In some places a man dresses up as a shrove-tide Tommy with his dirty Bet, a man in disguise. In Swiss and German villages they are nearer the original Wild Man with his Perchta or Berchta, the Bright One. Up in the sky now shines the wild hunter Orion, lumbering, awkward and sex-mad, after Diana the Bright One. Ripening in the orchards are the vegetables that trigger giggling: gourds, cucumbers, pumpkins, squashes raise their funny heads. Pie-scrambling, bottle-kicking and shrove-tide games of football mimic the hugging and tugging at the dead Sun of a lively archaic funeral. Men dress as women, because the Sun is now as potent as a female;

women as men, to shame him back to his role. Suppressed urges thaw and surface, now that the ice is cracking and snow is melting into slush, under a doddering Sun incapable of drying up the mud and the slime.

The ritual carnival pattern tells of Lucifer Morning Star first taking over and then giving way to the renewed Sun. On Sunday before Lent, hermaphrodite Venus, ruler of Pisces, arrives on her car, escorted by fishermen, transvestites and buffoons (opposite top r.), the retinue of Isis, the Moon, the Bright One, as described by Apuleius. Next she turns into, or is revealed to be, Lucifer of Shrove Tuesday. He displays his phallus, but gives birth to a baby. On Ash Wednesday he is killed, sometimes

consumed in the flames which symbolize the arrival of the fiery Ram, or the
Sun burning up his fake substitute, or his
self-sacrificing son, or the Sun doing
away with himself such as he was under
Pisces – a bleating, stumbling lamb. In
Spain Lucifer is sometimes represented
by an ass, which is tossed in the air and
will give birth to a truly solar horse.

At the centre of the whole show is
the male giving birth, displaying the
powers of the female. Only by positing a
male capable of giving birth can the
mystery of the origin – of the tribe, of
humanity, of the world, of the sun – be
solved. The primal ancestor can only be
a man in travail (opposite top l.). From
India (opposite top r.) to Italy (far left) the
scene is re-enacted, as if in answer to
the question in Jeremiah (30:5): 'Ask ye
now, and see whether a man doth
travail with child?'

Harlequin and Polichinello are connected with Carnival rites. They are
hermaphrodite lechers (above left) and
prankish mourners, who give birth to
children (left). Harlequin wears Hermes'
cap and brandishes a rod, a simplified
caduceus, which confers invisibility and
ubiquity, and opens up the world of the
dead. In Germanic lands he was said to
lead Diana's or Salomé-Herodias' (see p.
84) followers, the ribald army of the
dead, Harlequin's gang (the *maisnie
Harlequin* of Medieval France) on their
ecstatic Wild Hunt. Polichinello, dressed
in white like a dead child, headed the
set of stock characters, who with their

squeaky voices impersonated turkeys or
chicken, either strutting like cocks or
fluttering like hens. In Greece poultry
was the retinue of Proserpine (see p. 84).
The cock was Hermes' animal (see p. 77).

Carnivals seem to be stray threads
from the complex fabric of sorcery. In
Goya's painting the ass shows its head,
as it does at Spanish carnivals and at
Apuleius' feast of Isis, where it becomes
the Golden Ass. The two figures in the
foreground keep their heads covered,
like their counterparts at heathen sac-
rifices to the gods of the nether-world.
The witches wear Polichinello hats, the
same as are also worn by flagellants and
the victims of the Inquisition, and some
drug is sweeping them off their feet,
along with their delighted victim, who
seems to have completely lost her head
as she bends backwards (cf. pp. 84–85,
88–89) to be offered up to the Bright
One, whose light is flooding the group
soaring with her.

Left-hand page:
Pregnant male statue. Cameroon.
Collection M. Frederick Tristan, Paris.

Chauu dancer impersonating pregnant
woman in the dance of Kerala. India,
20th c.

Man giving birth. From Annabella Rossi
and R. de Simone, *Carnevale si chiamava
Vincenzo*, Rome, 1977.

Harlequin breastfeeds his son.
Engraving, Holland, 18th c. From P. L.
Duchartre, *La comédie italienne*, Paris,
1927.

Right-hand page:
Polichinella. Oil painting by Giovanni
Battista Tiepolo, Italy, 18th c. Ca'
Rezzonico, Venice.

Maskers of the Commedia del' Arte.
Victoria and Albert Museum, London.

Witches. Oil painting by Francisco de
Goya, Spain, 18th c. Ministerio de la
Gobernación, Madrid.

The bewitching androgyne

For the sake of their smooth, unremitting functioning, Western patriarchal societies have generally encouraged ideals of beauty that are uncompromisingly male or female. A change, however, was heralded by the writings of Johann Winckelmann at the end of the eighteenth century. In recent times the Western world has fallen back on his Classicist ideal whenever a restoration of 'sanity' and austerity in the arts has been attempted. But at a close inspection, Winckelmann's reaction against the Rococo in favour of 'simplicity and nature' shows itself to be a longing for androgyny; his Classicist taste was in fact born of a wild, epicene fervour. Beauty in the arts, he taught, is like tears on the stage, which lack realism unless an overbrimming imagination brings life to them; and the imagination he lavished on the cool beauty of the ancients was that of a compulsive lover of androgynes. To the replicas of Apollo and Dionysus that he imagined he met, he would quote Cowley's lines:

I thee both as man and woman prize,
For a perfect love implies
Love in all capacities.

(M. Praz, *On Neoclassicism*, London and Evanston, 1969.)

Arthur Atterley was the kind of androgyne beau that kindled the passions of the first Winckelmannian Classicists. He shows a cool eighteenth-century will to bewitch.

Friedrich Schlegel was, at the beginning of the nineteenth century, a most incredible forerunner of many trends that have been with us ever since. It was he who in art criticism first used the words 'modern' and 'interesting', instead of 'beautiful'. He suggested blending parody and earnestness, and mixing all literary genres together. He declared that fiction was henceforth going to dissect unnatural pleasures. In his novel *Lucinde* (1799) he commended fantasies of role-inversions in love. Why not explore, he asked, both man's cautious forcefulness and woman's alluring abandon, with the amusement of a child? Such playfulness, he added, was but the allegory, the mask for a mysterious archetypal human completeness, for the warmth of a love that is beyond man and woman.

His words set the pitch for Mademoiselle de Maupin (see p. 7), whose androgyne charm Beardsley's illustration seems to dissect as the result of her cold voluptuousness and theatri-

cal sweep. These traits are at the core of Colette's innocent-and-tainted explorations of sentimental borderlands. She loved to catch the glitter of androgyne tears and delighted to see how sleep could change her (female) friend into a Leonardesque St John the Baptist, just as Proust had felt an overwhelming rapture on seeing Albertine (his girl friend in his novel, his male chauffeur in real life) transmuted by slumber into a plant, into the infinite possibilities of life throbbing beneath closed eyelids. The cinema has duly turned all these themes into expendable myths, from the playfulness of transvestism combined with the 'puppet-complex' (far left), to all the haunting varieties of androgyne 'come hither' looks.

Concentration on androgyne hesitations and uncertainties might help the Western mind to overcome what James Hillman calls its 'extraverted' prejudice, which has inhibited Tantric and Taoist brands of eroticism. Such concentration certainly led Virginia Woolf to realize through the sexual ideal of Orlando (see also p. 9) that the I is but a figment, a free-floating delusion, which the exercise of a determined, unremitting sensitivity may finally dispel.

Left-hand page:
Jessie Matthews in 'First a Girl'. North America, 1936.

Mademoiselle de Maupin. Drawing by Aubrey Beardsley, for frontispiece of *Mademoiselle de Maupin*, 1898. Courtesy Fogg Art Museum, Grenville L. Winthrop Bequest, Cambridge (Mass.).

Vita Sackville-West as Orlando. From Virginia Woolf, *Orlando*, London, 1928.

Right-hand page:
Arthur Atterley as an Etonian. Oil painting by Sir Thomas Lawrence, England, 18th c. Los Angeles County Museum of Art.

Colette in 1904.

Marlene Dietrich off set.

Androgyne to angel

The Pharaoh Akhnaton is depicted offering libations to the sun-disc, Aton, followed by his wife and daughter. Rarely, even in Egypt, was androgyny stressed to such extremes. Velikovsky's idea that the legend of Oedipus might be based on a transposal to Thebes of the story of Akhnaton's reign in Egypt may seem shaky, but it does draw out certain features common to both stories, bringing into sharp focus the possibility that Aton, the 'god of the sun's disc', might be the answer to the riddle of the sphinx (see p. 19), since hieroglyphically the morning and the evening suns are represented by a child and by a man holding a cane within the sun's disc respectively. The essential activity of Aton, judging by the Pharaoh's hymn to him, seems to have been the quickening of embryos. Androgyny was the aim of various Egyptian initiation ceremonies, such as putting on the holy garment and 'passing through the skin', which was a return to the embryo. The plunge into the pool of the seven stars (*Book of the Dead*, XCVII–XCVIII) made the adept androgyne like a god. The Pharaoh was especially androgyne, his female wisdom symbolized by the cobra goddess of wisdom poised upon his forehead, while his phallus symbolized military prowess. Akhnaton's breasts and large hips stressed his androgyne

nature, and his elongated, ethereal limbs and frail-wristed, upward-curving hands seem to imply that he is being transformed into an angel.

Eros-Hermaphroditus was associated with flowers, shells and eggs. It has been suggested that Eros and Psyche were originally (or ideally) one. The angelic, winged, delicate creative urge in nature was visualized as the blending of the two demi-gods in one. The same idea is expressed in alchemy: an angelic mercurial androgyne *homunculus* rises from the androgynization. Balzac's *Séraphitus* (see also p. 7) illustrates the androgyne's ascent from nature to the realm of angels. Séraphitus (below right) hovers above cloying human passions, his remote sweetness is both adolescent and fatherly. The sharp power of the eagle and the languor of the turtle-dove both resound in his voice, his long diaphanous hands can grip like the pincers of a crab, his is the stern quality of a warrior angel. He answers to the vision in *Revelation* 14:4, 'These are they that were not defiled with women; for they are maidens'. It is as his feminine double (opposite above) that he appears in the final scene as heaven-ascending Séraphita.

Youths interpreting supernatural female beings often exhibit a distillation of female charm, as though drawing from the depths of their being a vivid

image of their female guardian. The Chinese actor trailing sashes like clouds, pointing to beyondness, is an ideal impersonation of the original characters from which the personality of the heavenly nymph of the Chinese stage derived – the shaman-maidens who danced, dipping and leaping like kingfishers, to raise from the realms of possible perfection the 'long-limbed and sinuous' otherworldly spirits (Wilson 1980).

Left-hand page:
King Akhnaton offering libations to the sun. Indurated limestone relief from Amarna, Egypt, 14th c. BC.

Eros-Hermaphroditus. Terracotta figurine, Greece, 4th c. BC. British Museum, London.

Séraphitus. Engraving by G. Staal from Honoré de Balzac, *Oeuvres illustrées*, Paris, 1851–55. British Library, London.

Right-hand page:
Séraphita. Engraving by G. Staal from Honoré de Balzac, *Oeuvres illustrées*, Paris, 1851–55. British Library, London.

Mei Lan-fang as the heavenly maiden. From *Mei Lan-fang, Foremost Actor of China*, Shanghai, 1929.

Alchemical androgynization. Ms. illustration from Arnold of Villanova, *Rosarium philosophorum*, Ms. 394a, 16th c. Stadbibliothek Vadiana, St Gallen.

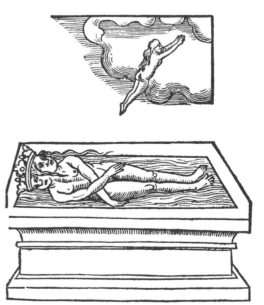

Sources

Bagatti, B., 'La mitica rigenerazione della vita in un amuleto samaritano-cristiano del IV secolo', in *Liber annuus*, XXIII (1973), Jerusalem, 1973.

Baumann, H., *Das doppelte Geschlecht*, Berlin, 1955, pp. 41–81.

Bausani, A., in *L'Oriente cristiano*, Rome, 1964, pp. 153ff.

Behmen [Boehme], J., *Von der Gnadenwahl*, 1623, also published in *Theosophische Werken*, Amsterdam, 1682 (5:35).

Bichen, Z., *Traité d'alchimie et de physiologie taoïste (Weisheng Shenlixue mingzhi)*, ed. C. Despeux, Paris, 1979.

Blofeld, J., *Compassion Yoga*, Winchester (Mass.), 1978; London, 1979.

Bourignon, A., *Toutes les oeuvres*, Amsterdam, 1679–86.

Bruno, G., *Jordani Bruni Nolani opera latine conscripta*, Naples, 1884.

Busson, Abbé, 'L'Origine égyptienne de la kabbale' pt 2, in *Compte rendu du Troisième Congrès Scientifique International des Catholiques*, Brussels, 1895, p. 74.

Chen, C. M., *Discriminations*, Republic of China, 1968.

Colin, J., 'Juvenal et le mariage mystique de Gracchus', in *Atti Accad. delle scienze*, XC, Turin, 1956.

Daniélou, A., *Le Polythéisme indien*, Paris, 1960 (English trs.: *Hindu Polytheism*, London and New York, 1964).

Dobbs, B. J. T., *The Foundations of Newton's Alchemy, or The Hunting of the Greene Lyon*, Cambridge and New York, 1975.

D'Onofrio, C., *La Papessa Giovanna*, Rome, 1979.

Drower, R. S., *The Secret Adam: A Study in Naṣorean Gnosis*, Oxford, 1960.

Emerson, R. W., *Brahma*, in *Complete Works*, Boston and London, 1903–04.

Fasce, S., *Eros: la figura e il culto* (with bibliography), Genoa, 1977.

Foigny, G. de, *La Terre australe connue*, Geneva, 1676. English trs.: *A New Discovery of Terra Incognita Australis, or The Southern World, by James Sadeur, a French-man*, London, 1693.

Frazão, S., *Estudos etnogràficos dos povos de Angola*, Lisbon, 1946, pp. 159ff.

Gulik, R. H. van, *Sexual Life in Ancient China*, Leiden, 1961.

Halifax, J., *Shamanic Voices*, New York, 1979.

Hevajra Tantra, The, ed. D. L. Snellgrove, London and New York, 1959.

Hutin, S., *Les Disciples anglais de Jacob Boehme*, Paris, 1960.

Johanaan, J. D., (ed.), *Joseph and Potiphar's Wife*, New York, 1968.

Jung, C. G., 'Mysterium coniunctionis', XII: 3, in *Collected Works*, XIV, Princeton, 1970–71; London, 1970.

Lai, T. C., *The Eight Immortals*, Hong Kong, 1972.

Layard, J., *The Virgin Archetype*, Zurich, 1972, 1977; Irving (Tex.), 1973, 1977.

Lu K'uan Yü, *Taoist Yoga: Alchemy and Immortality*, London, 1970.

Midrash Rabbah, English trs. by H. Freedman and M. Simmons, 1–9, London, 1939.

Miller, D. A., 'Royauté et ambiguïté sexuelle', in *Annales*, May-August 1971, Paris, 1971.

Noskham, 'Nyingma Teachings on the Intermediate Stage', in *Creative Spaces*, January 1976, Manchester, 1976.

Patai, R., *The Hebrew Goddess*, New York, 1978, p. 139.

——, *The Jewish Mind*, New York, 1977, ch. 6.

Pittaluga, M., 'Immagini e simboli del mito postelliano', in *Il superuomo e i suoi simboli nelle letterature moderne*, ed. E. Zolla, VI, Florence, 1979.

Robinson, J. M., (ed.), *The Nag Hammadi Library*, New York, 1977.

Saunders, E. Dale, *Mūdrā*, New York and London, 1960, pp. 59–60.

Scholem, G. G., 'La Symbolique des couleurs dans la tradition mystique juive' pt 2, in *Diogène*, CIX, Paris, 1980.

Schulman, D., *Tamil Temple Myths*, Princeton, 1977.

Signorini, I., 'The Marriage Between Persons of the Same Sex among the Nzema of Southwestern Ghana', in *Journal de la société des africanistes*, XLIII, 2, Paris, 1973.

Singer, J., *Androgyny: Towards a New Theory of Sexuality*, New York, 1976, London 1977.

Snellgrove, D. L. (ed.), *The Hevajra Tantra*, London and New York, 1959.

Stokes, A., *The Critical Writings of Adrian Stokes*, London and New York, 1978.

Testa, P., *Il simbolismo dei giudeo-cristiani*, Jerusalem, 1962.

Ummu'l Kitab (text, with Italian trs. and commentary by P. Filippani-Ronconi), Naples, 1966, p. 273.

Wilson, P. L., *Angels*, London and New York, 1980, p. 166ff.

Acknowledgments

The objects in the text and plates, pp. 4–64, are in the collections of:

Biblioteca Ambrosiana, Milan 56; Bibliothèque de l'Arsenal, Paris 40; Bibliothèque Nationale, Paris 48–49, 63; British Museum, London 4, 61; M. H. de Young Memorial Museum, Fine Arts Museums of San Francisco 57; The Dean and Chapter of Westminster, London 26; Galleria degli Uffizi, Florence 52; Mr and Mrs H. Lenart, Los Angeles County Museum of Art 59; Musei Vaticani, Rome 58; Museo Barracco, Rome 54; Museum Boymans-van Beuningen, Rotterdam 44; Museum of Modern Art, New York 62; National Museum of History, T'aipei 17; New York Public Library, Library and Museum of the Performing Arts, Dance Collection (photo Baron Adolphe de Meyer) 55; private collection 46; private collection, Paris 53; Tokyo University of Fine Arts 37.

Photographs were supplied by:

Alinari 54, 72 above, 77, 88 above l.; Bayerische Staaatsbibliothek, Munich 79 below r.; Brian Beresford 33; Albert Bonniers Förlag, Stockholm (photos Lennart Nilsson, from his book *A Child is Born*, Faber and Faber, London 1977, Delacorte Press/Seymour Lawrence, New York 1977) 36, 39; British Museum, London 94 below l.; Christie's 60; David Finn 89 below; Fogg Art Museum, Harvard University 92 below l.; Werner Forman 64, 74 below l.; Fotografia Giacomelli 90 above r.; Hirmer Foto Archiv 94 above; Jacqueline Hyde 90 above l.; John Kobal Collection 50, 92 above, 93 below r.; Francette Levieux 73 below l.; Los Angeles County Museum of Art 93 above; Mansell Collection 93 below l.; MAS 91 below; Mesa Verde National Park Museum 83 above l.; Musée de l'Homme, Paris 74 above; Museum of Mankind, London 67 centre; Museum of the American Indian, Heye Foundation, New York 82 r.; Nationalmuseum, Stockholm 75 l.; Phaidon Press Ltd 86 below; Axel Poignant 67 below l.; By Gracious Permission of H.M. the Queen 84 below, 88 below r.; RCA Records (photo Brian Ward) 51; Mick Rock 47; Ann Ronan Picture Library 74 below r.; Scala 52; Science Museum, London 35; Edwin Smith, 91 above l.; Smithsonian Institution, Washington DC 82 l.; Studio Fontanelli 41; Jeff Teasdale 66 above l. and below, 67 below r., 68 above, 73 below r., 85 below l.; Victoria and Albert Museum, London 91 above r.; Zentralbibliothek, Zürich 45.